D1432752

Social Literacies

Real Language Series

General Editors:
Jennifer Coates, Roehampton Institute, London
Jenny Cheshire, Universities of Fribourg and Neuchâtel,
and
Euan Reid, Institute of Education, University of London

Titles published in the series:

David Lee Competing Discourses: Perspective and Ideology in Language
Norman Fairclough (Editor) Critical Language Awareness
James Milroy and Lesley Milroy (Editors) Real English: The Grammar of English Dialects in the British Isles
Mark Sebba London Jamaican: Language Systems in Interaction
Janet Holmes Women, Men and Politeness
Ben Rampton Crossing: Language and Ethnicity Among Adolescence
Brian V. Street Social Literacies: Critical Approaches to Literacy in Development, Ethnography and Education

Social Literacies:
Critical Approaches to Literacy in
Development, Ethnography and Education

Brian V. Street

LONGMAN
London and New York

Longman Group Limited,
Longman House, Burnt Mill,
Harlow, Essex CM20 2JE, England
and Associated Companies throughout the world.

*Published in the United States of America
by Longman Publishing, New York*

© Longman Group Limited 1995

First published 1995

ISBN 0 582 102200 CSD
ISBN 0 582 102219 PPR

British Library Cataloguing-in-Publication Data

A catalogue record for this book is
available from the British Library

Library of Congress Cataloging-in-Publication Data
Street, Brian V.
 Social literacies: critical approaches to literacy development,
  ethnography, and education/ Brian V. Street.
 p. cm. — (Real language series)
 Includes bibliographical references and index.
 ISBN 0–582–10220–0. — ISBN 0–582–10221–9 (paper)
 1. Literacy. 2. Critical pedagogy. I. Title. II. Series.
LC149.S78 1995
302.2'244—dc20   94–38385
                                                                CIP

Produced by Longman Singapore Publishers (Pte) Ltd. Printed
in Singapore

Set by 15R in 10/12pt Monophoto Sabon

Contents

To My Mother, Margaret Street
and
In Memory of My Father, Harry Street

Acknowledgements

We are indebted to the following copyright holders for permission to reproduce previously published articles by the author:

Deakin University for 'Putting Literacies in the Political Agenda' in *Open Letter*: Australian Journal for Adult Literacy Research and Practice, vol. 1, no. 1, 1990; Ithaca Press for 'The Uses of Literacy and Anthropology in Iran' in *The Diversity of the Muslim Community* ed. A. Al-Shahi; Museum Tusculanums Forlag for 'Orality and Literacy as Ideological Constructions' in *Culture and History*, vol. 2; Pergamon Press Ltd for 'Literacy and Social Change: the significance of social context in the development of literacy programmes' in *The Future of Literacy in a Changing World* (1988) ed. D. Wagner; Sage Publications Inc for 'The Schooling of Literacy' (with J. Street) in *Writing in the Community* (1990) ed. D. Barton and R. Ivanic; Springer Press for 'Literacy Practices and Literacy Myths' in *The Written Word* (1988) ed. R. Saljo; University of Pennsylvania for 'A Critical Look at Walter Ong and the "Great Divide"' in *Literacy Research Newsletter* vol. 4, no. 1, spring 1988.

Introduction

There has been a significant increase in scholarly concern with literacy from a theoretical and cross-cultural perspective in recent years. Previously, the focus of much academic research was upon cognitive conseqences of literacy acquisition. In sociolinguistics the emphasis has been on the differences between literacy and orality as channels of communication and in educational contexts upon 'problems' of acquisition and how to 'remediate' learners with reading and writing difficulties. Recently, however, the trend has been towards a broader consideration of literacy as a social practice and in a cross-cultural perspective. Within this framework an important shift has been the rejection by many writers of the dominant view of literacy as a 'neutral', technical skill, and the conceptualization of literacy instead as an ideological practice, implicated in power relations and embedded in specific cultural meanings and practices – what I have described as the 'New Literacy Studies' (cf. Street, 1993a and b; cf. also Gee, 1990). From this perspective the relationship between written and oral language differs according to context – there is no one universal account of 'the oral' and 'the written'. Social and material conditions affect (if not determine) the significance of a given form of communication and it is inappropriate, if not impossible, to read off from the channel what will be either the cognitive processes employed or the functions to which the communicative practice is put.

The field of Literacy Studies can be characterized at present as being in a transitional phase. The new theoretical perspectives are affecting practical programmes unevenly, while the experience of on-the-ground practitioners is feeding differentially into academic research. The present book attempts an overview and a unifying perspective on these developments, addressing a range of literacy sectors; commencing with arguments about the political nature of literacy in development programmes; citing case studies from my own anthropological field-work in Iran during the 1970s and offering some re-analysis of ethnographic approaches to the study of literacy; providing a further case study from more recent ethnographic studies of literacy and schooling in the USA and considering some contemporary thinking in education; and finally offering a critical framework for further research and practical work in literacy.

The book is entitled 'Social Literacies', in order to emphasize the focus of these new approaches, first on the *social* nature of literacy and secondly on the multiple character of literacy practices. This, then, challenges the dominant emphasis on a single, 'neutral' 'Literacy' with a big 'L' and a single 'y'. To describe the specificity of literacies in particular places and times, I have found it helpful to employ the concept of 'literacy practices' which is a development from Heath's concept of 'literacy events' (see chapter 8, 'Literacy Practices and Literacy Myths'). 'Literacy events' for Heath refer to 'any occasion in which a piece of writing is integral to the nature of the participants' interactions and their interpretative processes' (Heath, 1982). The concept of 'Literacy practices' is pitched at a higher level of abstraction and refers to both behaviour and the social and cultural conceptualizations that give meaning to the uses of reading and/or writing. Literacy practices incorporate not only 'literacy events', as empirical occasions to which literacy is integral, but also folk models of those events and the ideological preconceptions that underpin them. David Barton compares my usage to that of Scribner and Cole, who, 'coming from a psychological perspective . . . developed a "practice account" of literacy'. He argues for some combination of these meanings and for continued use of both concepts: 'Literacy *events* are the particular activities in which literacy has a role: they may be regular repeated activities. Literacy *practices* are the general cultural ways of utilizing literacy that people draw upon in a literacy event' (Barton, 1991, p. 5). Grillo (1989), adopting my earlier interpretation of literacy as 'shorthand for the social practices of reading and writing' (Street, 1984, p. 1), argues that 'literacy is seen as one type of communicative practice' (Grillo, 1989, p. 8): he locates the study of literacy in the broader context of the ethnographic study of communicative practices in different social contexts (cf. Hymes, 1974). It is in these senses, then, that this volume is concerned with 'Social Literacies'.

One of the major issues raised in these discussions concerns the ways in which we can move the study of literacy away from idealized generalization about the nature of Language and of Literacy and towards more concrete understanding of literacy practices in 'real' social contexts. The approach to literacy practices in the present volume, then, represents a particular view of the notion of 'real language' exemplified by the series as a whole. That is, reading and writing are here located within the real social and linguistic practices that give them meaning, rather than, as is the case with much sociolinguistic convention, illustrated through hypothetical examples or, as in much educational discourse, represented in idealized and prescriptive terms. I shall occasionally illustrate the argument by reference to 'real' examples of texts and documents – invoices and bills collected during my field-work in an Iranian village; texts used to test adult basic literacy in the USA; love poems inscribed on bamboo or palm leaves in South-East Asia. But the argument proceeds mainly through accounts of the social practices of reading and writing in context, and of variation in the uses and meanings of literacy in different cultural settings and within different academic discourses – critical, educational, developmental and ethnographic. The focus on context, then, is what makes the Literacy Practices described here 'real'.

It is an irony of recent sociolinguistic study that, while there has indeed been a move towards real language in the study of oral performance, there is still a tendency to reify written language and to accept the grand claims of the educationalists and developers in this area while emphasizing diversity and complexity in the spoken channel. Debbie Cameron, for instance, develops the 'Real Language' approach in one of the most influential books of the last decade, *Feminism and Linguistic Theory*. She emphasizes strongly actual social practice and context with respect to language in general, but she has a tendency to slip back into some of the reified abstractions of the autonomous model of literacy (see chapter 2 below) when she addresses literacy specifically. She cites traditional exponents of the 'autonomous' model such as Walter Ong (see chapter 7 below) and John Oxenham (1980), uncritically: 'the more literate people are, the more willing they are to accept and work for improvements in their societies . . . They become more willing to reason for themselves, less willing to take opinions on authority' (Oxenham, 1980, p. 51; cited in Cameron, 1985, p. 147). These are precisely the sort of assumptions being challenged in the New Literacy Studies and it is indicative of the state of thinking about literacy in sociolinguistics that a progressive and radical sociolinguist should still give them credence while challenging traditional assumptions about language in general.

Indeed, much linguistic writing about literacy has been dominated by the traditional and somewhat reified debate about the relationship between written language and speech. Halliday, for instance, argues that spoken and written language differ in fundamental ways; he contrasts the prosodic features and grammatical intricacy of speech with the high lexical density and grammatical metaphor of writing (Halliday, 1985). He uses evolutionary and functional arguments to support this point. Writing, he argues, has evolved differently from spoken language because it fulfils different functions. While agreeing with Halliday in his concern to trace developments and changes in written and oral language (cf. Graff, 1987; Clanchy, 1979; Halliday and Martin, 1993), his focus on evolution and on function tend to ring warning bells, particularly for anthropologists. Anthropologists have long been critical of evolutionary explanations, of the kind popular during the last century (cf. Stocking, 1968), for being speculative and removed from real historical time into a distant past about which we can know little – especially about the uses of written and spoken language. The idea of evolution has a universalizing tendency: it does not to help us explain why and how specific differences between written and spoken language have emerged and have been reproduced in given contexts. Similarly, the idea that writing emerged to fulfil different 'functions' from speech seems rather essentialist: it does not fit well with the growing empirical evidence of variation between cultures and historical periods. More generally, the theoretical assumption that social facts can be explained with reference to their 'functions' – that they fulfil 'needs' – has been questioned in anthropology (where it was very popular for a number of years). One problem is its circularity: how do we know there is a need for it? – because it has evolved to fulfil this need; how do we know it has evolved for this purpose? – because that is what it does now. There is also a homeostatic quality about functional explanations which lead them to accept current classifications and social forms rather than asking how they were specifically produced, through what ideological and discursive formations and how are they reproduced against competing forms. Asad (1980) suggests we should ask not what are the 'essential meanings' in a given culture, but how do specific meanings claim authority against competing ones and how are these marginalized? The problem with functional explanation in his own discipline, social anthropology, has been that: 'Instead of taking the production of essential meanings (in the form of authoritative discourse) in given historical societies as the problem to be explained, anthropology has taken the existence of essential meanings (in the form of "authentic discourse") as the basic concept for defining and explaining historical societies' (1980, p. 623). A similar charge could be levelled at much of the linguistic theory about the differences between spoken and written language.

I will consider here a further example of the different ways in which this argument is approached in order to illustrate the nature of the New Literacy Studies and what I mean by applying the notion of 'Real Language' to the study of literacy practices. Deborah Tannen has attempted to develop a more sophisticated view of the social differences between written and spoken language than that offered by a functional approach but, as I argue in more detail in chapter 8, she does nevertheless reproduce features of an older 'great divide' tradition. She claims that a greater degree of 'involvement' is to be found in oral language as opposed to the 'detachment' found in the written medium (Tannen, 1982). Since writing lacks the paralinguistic channels available in face-to-face speech interactions, it is obliged to encode meaning only lexically and syntactically. Ethnographers such as Shuman (1986) and Besnier (1988), who are considered in more detail below, point out, to the contrary, that writing does involve many paralinguistic features, equivalent in some ways to the gesture, facial expression, intonation of spoken language – the choice of type or script, ink colour, publishing signs such as hard covers, etc., all signify meaning beyond lexical and syntactic means. If there are universal differences in channel, despite the growing evidence, it will be difficult to identify if we already presume such difference in the model of language we use in the first place: i.e., if we assume features of 'writing' and then, when we find these features in speech, call them 'writing-like' then the argument is circular and cannot be tested. Tannen's continued discovery of 'oral-like' features in writing and 'written-like' features in speech make one wonder why these features of communicative practice had to be labelled by channel in the first place.

I will use one recent example of the application of these ideas and labels to educational research and pedagogy, in order to indicate, some of the problems that occur when these models of language and literacy are put to work in 'real' situations. Jennifer Hammond (1990) draws explicitly on Halliday in addressing the question for teachers in Australian primary schools, 'Is learning to read and write the same as learning to speak?'. She argues that it is not the same. Like Halliday, she describes the differences between the channels in terms of prosodic, lexical and grammatical features, also suggesting like Tannen that written language is by nature less contextualized and less interactive: since 'the writer cannot depend on a shared context to convey any of the meaning ... the meaning must be contained within the text itself. Spoken text, on the other hand, is "dialogic in nature" ' (1990, p. 32). There seem to be times when she and other writers in this genre treat the differences that students are learning as though they are not a culture-specific set of conventions but a general feature of reading and writing in themselves. Hammond, for instance, seems to suggest that the characteristics she finds for written language and spoken language in the Australian classrooms she researched are somehow general to the channels rather than conventional to this context. 'A more conscious, deliberate and analytic effort is involved in learning to read and write than in learning to speak' (p. 51). While agreeing that 'A "fresh look" at literacy must acknowledge differences as well as similarities between learning to speak and learning to read and write', and recognizing the importance of high-quality research such as Hammond's that draws attention to linguistic aspects of child learning, I would want to give greater attention to the cultural nature of these processes. The differences that researchers and teachers identify are constructed and valued in specific contexts: schooling (and research) itself contributes to their creation and reproduction. A Critical Language Awareness approach, of the kind advocated by Fairclough (1992) and others would put the question of the cultural construction of difference on to the educational agenda, rather than taking differences between speech and writing as given universals. As I suggest in chapter 6, the implications of the New Literacy Studies for pedagogy are that we need to move beyond teaching children about the technical features of language 'functions' and help them instead towards awareness of the socially and ideologically constructed nature of the specific forms we inhabit and use at given times.

An approach to pedagogy of this kind needs to be grounded, then, in new theories of language and literacy and in new methods for studying them. A number of the writers cited in the essays in this volume indicate what work such as this might look like and how it might be usefully applied. Shuman (1986), for instance, working within the Ethnography of Communication tradition in the USA, has addressed similar questions regarding the characteristics of written and spoken language to those raised by the linguists cited above, but has come to quite different conclusions. Her work demonstrates how assumptions about what belongs to each mode – spoken and written – are challenged by fine-grained ethnographic accounts of actual practices – 'Real Language'. She describes the uses of writing and speech among adolescents at a Philadelphia High School to demonstrate that features of discourse traditionally attributed to writing – such as 'distancing' – may be found in oral interactions ('he said she said' etc.), while features of discourse often attributed to speech – such as 'proximity' – are to be found in written interactions (e.g., editing of written drafts of rap songs). Besnier (1988) recounts the differences that have been claimed between writing and speech and concludes that once close ethnographic accounts are analyzed, few general differences remain. Not only is the idea of a 'great divide' between writing and speech untenable, but he suggests, citing Biber's (1988) large corpus study of variation across speech and writing, even the notion of a 'uni-dimensional continuum is inadequate to accommodate the variations in linguistic behaviour across contexts of oral and written communication' (in Besnier and Street, 1994). He argues, with respect to his own anthropological field-work among Tuvaluan speakers in the South Pacific region, that, contrary to many claims made for English 'and tacitly for speaking and writing in general, spoken Tuvaluan is not necessarily more involved and less complex, and more context-dependent than written Tuvaluan'. More generally, 'the structural characteristics of each register do not depend on whether it is produced in the spoken or written mode ... The structural patterns found in this study do not support the view that spoken language is more involved, more interactive, and less complex than written language' (1988, p. 710). These characterstics are instead viewed as dependent upon the communicative norms at play in each register. The structured relationships of spoken and written language must be explained in terms of the social context of orality and literacy in different literacy traditions, rather than the cognitive demands of language production or isolated (universal) structural features of the spoken and written modes.

The research models that Besnier critiques have themselves served to create and reproduce the differences between reading and writing that are currently treated as 'natural' in both academic and popular discourses. If we take the differences as given and then research the details, we are failing to give sufficient credit to the broader 'context' of time and place in which these details occur and out of which our own models have grown. If we start instead with language and discourse as social practices and then ask how particular conventions are created and reproduced in specific contexts, we might find there are situations where focus on the differences between speech and writing is not relevant to our understanding of the situation. To take seminars for instance: we speak, take notes, read from previously produced text, read notes silently and aloud, borrow discourse genres from the note form, lectures and books while writing in conventions associated with the oral interactions we are engaged in: the whole is in some way greater than the sum of its parts and it is more meaningful to address this unit than to break it down into components that may have a different significance here than they do when they occur as part of other wholes elsewhere. The traditional emphasis among linguists on the differences between speech and writing is, then, challenged both theoretically and methodologically by the social view of language being developed here. The study of literacy practices begins with a different agenda and conceptualizes and investigates the relationship between language, literacy and society differently.

The use of more socially focused approaches for purposes of specific analyses within this book are intended to help develop and consolidate these new understandings of literacy practices and to apply them to specific 'real' situations. The four Sections – 'Literacy, Politics and Social Change', 'The Ethnography of Literacy', 'Literacy in Education' and 'Towards a Critical Framework' – focus on different aspects of literacy studies and aim to offer the reader a guide through the argument as a whole, concluding with Section 4 that offers a theoretical framework for further work in the light of the critique of earlier approaches. An Introduction to each Section put the papers into contemporary perspective, but I have not extensively re-written those that have been previously published, apart from changes to take account of period, discrepancies and repetition and to locate them in their sequence in the book. Inevitably, many retain the distinctive character of the purpose for which they were originally written – for example chapter 1 was written as a critique of the representations of literacy that persisted through International Literacy Year, 1990, and that I argue are still prevalant today; while chapter 5 was written in the USA in the late 1980s as an attempt to apply the new theoretical and methodological perspectives to classroom and community practices there and to popular debates about literacy at that time.

Taken in sequence, the chapters do, however, constitute a cohesive whole in terms of the (developing) argument and its application to these different domains. The introduction at the beginning of each section establishes its relationship to the central themes and concepts of the book as a whole and summarizes each chapter in that section in the light of my present argument. The first Section attempts to link specific insights regarding literacy practices to broader cultural and policital debates, thereby addressing the interest of the Real Language series in 'the relationship between language and social change'. The second Section provides specific ethnographic accounts of literacy practices, both from my own anthropological field-work in Iran and from a selection of recent ethnography. The third Section builds on these case studies, developing the theoretical arguments in the context of Education and testing them out in relation to classroom practice. Ethnographic approaches to the study of language in Education have, of course, been popular for some time (cf. Stubbs, 1986), especially in the USA, but again their application to literacy practices is more recent and their value in the broader context of development politics and of educational policy is only recently being recognized. The final Section brings together the assumptions and concepts employed in the earlier Sections and proposes a critical framework for further study.

References

Asad, T. (1980) 'Anthropology and the Analysis of Ideology', *Man*, n.s., vol. 14, no. 4.

Barton, D. (1991) 'The Social Nature of Writing', in D. Barton and R. Ivanic (eds) *Writing in the Community*. Sage: London.

Besnier, N. (1988) 'The Linguistic Relationship of Spoken and Written Nukulaelae Registers', *Language*, vol. 64, no. 4.

Besnier, N. and Street, B. (1994) 'Aspects of Literacy', in T. Ingold (ed.) *Companion Encyclopedia of Anthropology*. Routledge: London.

Biber, D. (1988) *Variation Across Speech and Writing*. CUP: Cambridge.

Cameron, D. (1985) *Feminism and Linguistic Theory*. Macmillan: London.

Clanchy, M. (1979) *From Memory to Written Record: England 1066–1307*. Edward Arnold: London.

Fairclough, N. (ed.) (1992) *Critical Language Awareness*. Longman: London.

Fishman, J. (1986) 'Nationality-nationalism and Nation-nationism', in J. Fishman, C. Ferguson and J. Das Gupta (eds) *Language Problems of Developing Nations*. John Wiley: New York.

Gee, J. (1990) *Social Linguistics and Literacies: Ideology in Discourses*. Falmer Press: Brighton.

Graff, H. (1987) *The Legacies of Literacy: Continuities and Contradictions in Western Culture and Society*. Indiana University Press: Bloomington, Indiana.

Grillo, R. (1989) *Dominant Languages*. CUP: Cambridge.

Halliday, M.K. (1985) *Spoken and Written Language*. OUP: Oxford.

Halliday, M.K. and Martin, J. (1993) *Writing Science: Literacy and Discursive Power*. Falmer Press: London.

Hammond, J. (1990) 'Is Learning to Read and Write the Same as Learning to Speak?', in F. Christie (ed.) *Literacy for a Changing World*. Falmer Press: London.

Heath, S.B. (1982) 'What No Bedtime Story Means: Narrative Skills at Home and at School', *Language in Society*, vol 11: 49–76.

Hymes, D. (1974) *Foundations in Sociolinguistics: an Ethnographic Approach*. University of Pennsylvania Press: Philadelphia.

Oxenham, J. (1980) *Literacy: Writing, Reading and Social Organisation*. Routledge & Kegan Paul: London.

Shuman, A. (1986) *Storytelling Rights: the Uses of Oral and Written Texts by Urban Adolescents*. CUP: Cambridge.

Stocking, G. (1968) *Race, Culture and Evolution*. Free Press: New York.

Street, B. (1984) *Literacy in Theory and Practice*. CUP: Cambridge.

Street, B. (ed.) (1993a) *Cross-Cultural Approaches to Literacy*. CUP: Cambridge.

Street, B. (1993b) 'The New Literacy Studies', *Journal of Research in Reading*, vol. 16, no. 2: 81–97. Blackwell: Oxford.

Stubbs, M. (1986) *Educational Linguistics*. Basil Blackwell: Oxford.

Tannen, D. (1982) 'The Myth of Orality and Literacy', in W. Frawley (ed.) *Linguistics and Literacy*. Plenum: New York.

Section 1:

Literacy, Politics and Social Change

Introduction

The first Section attempts to link specific insights regarding literacy practices to broader cultural and political debates, thereby addressing the interest of the Real Language series in 'the relationship between language and social change'. In the transmission of literacy to so-called 'developing' societies, many of the assumptions of the culture. and literacy bearers have been premised upon what I term an 'autonomous' model of literacy and against which I have proposed an 'ideological' model. This section attempts to bring out the implications of this framework of thought for particular campaigns and suggests ways in which the relationship between literacy and culture can be re-thought within the literacy programmes of the 1990s.

Chapter 1: Putting Literacies on the Political Agenda

This chapter arose out of dissatisfaction with the representations of literacy evident in Agency and media accounts during International Literacy Year (1990). The rhetoric intended to draw public attention to literacy and to encourage both financial and organizational resources into the field, reproduced many of the stereotypes of the autonomous model: in particular, that 'illiterates' were lacking in cognitive skills, living in 'darkness' and 'backward' and that the acquisition of literacy would (in itself, 'autonomously') lead to major 'impacts' in terms of social and cognitive skills and 'Development'. While such claims may achieve the short-term aim of shocking the public and governments into some response, in the long term it is likely to be damaging to the field, both in the ways in which it demeans those adults who do have literacy difficulties and also because it raises false expectations of what they and their society can expect once they do improve literacy skills.

Statements by developers regarding the need for literacy, the importance of literacy for development and the terrible consequences of 'illiteracy', all assume that we know what 'literacy' is and that when people acquire it they will somehow 'get better'. I argue that behind these assumptions is usually a very western-oriented and narrow image of what 'literacy' is, a model based upon the particular uses and associations of literacy in recent European and North American history. I suggest that these narrow assumptions about literacy might provide an explanation for the failure of so many literacy campaigns in recent years. They have involved the construction of a 'stigma' of illiteracy where many people had operated in the oral domain without feeling that it was a problem. Where this has happened, the concept of 'illiteracy' has itself become one of the major problems in people's ability to see themselves as communicators. The rhetoric of public campaigns reinforces rather than challenges these images. International Literacy Year should have been used to open up these debates and to establish clear frameworks and concepts on which programmes can be based, not to reiterate worn clichés and patronizing stories about 'illiteracy'. The new thinking about literacy outlined in this book might, I suggest, provide a more fruitful framework for future action and campaigns. This involves recognizing the multiplicity of literacy practices rather than assuming a single Literacy has to be transferred in every Literacy Campaign. It also assumes that questions regarding which literacy is appropriate for a given context and campaign is itself a political question, not simply a matter of neutral choice by technical 'experts'. In this sense, 'Putting Literacies on the Political Agenda' is the first task of Development Agencies and of Educationalists. It is to this challenge that the energy and stimulus of International Literacy work should be addressed.

Chapter 2: Literacy and Social Change: The Significance of Social Context in the Development of Literacy Programmes

This chapter argues that the transfer of literacy from a dominant group to those who previously had little experience of reading and writing, involves more than simply the passing on of some technical, surface skills. Rather, for those receiving the new literacy, the impact of the culture and of the politico-economic structures of those bringing it is likely to be more significant than the impact of the technical skills associated with reading and writing. The shifts in meaning associated with such transfers are located at deep, epistemological levels, raising quesons about what is truth, what is knowledge and what are appropriate sources of authority. Clanchy (1979), for instance, reports how the apparently simple act of dating a business letter in medieval England had profound significance of a religious and doctrinal kind: for a secular person to locate themselves in a time frame that was essentially non-secular was seen as sacrilege, a profanity, not merely a technical matter of learning conventions for different genres of writing. I explore this material in some detail as it is sufficiently distanced from immediate pressures and significance to serve as an exemplar for much contemporary practice in development campaigns for literacy. The changes being wrought by a present-day literacy programme may likewise strike deep at the roots of cultural belief, a fact that may go unnoticed within a framework that assumes that reading and writing are simply technical skills. The medieval example, rooted in the changes brought by the conquering Normans to Anglo-Saxon England, also brings out the extent to which power relations, often of a colonial kind, underlie many literacy programmes. There too, as in many modern cases, the indigenous population had literacy practices of its own that were undervalued and marginalized by the standard being introduced. People are not 'tabula rasa', waiting for the novel imprint of literacy, as many campaigns seem to assume. The uses of oral conventions for memorizing, asserting authority and claiming rights are able to achieve the objectives that colonists and educators have claimed could only be accomplished by the written word: indeed, in the case of medieval England, the local population were acutely aware of how susceptible to forgery and deception was the written word, especially in the hands of conquerors eager to assert claims to land they had newly acquired. Claims for the neutral and objective character of writing were seen for the political self-interest they clearly were.

Similar processes can be observed in many modern contexts where literacy is brought by outsiders. Claims for the consequence of literacy are frequently couched in the neutral language of 'objective' science while disguising the political and economic interests of those imparting it. I explore these power relations, as they are implicated in literacy campaigns in a number of developing countries and make a working distinction between 'colonial' literacy – brought by outsiders as part of a conquest – and 'dominant' literacy – brought by members of the same society but frequently belonging to different classes, ethnic groups or localities. Describing case studies from Malagasy, Iran and India, I argue for a more culturally sensitive analysis of literacy transfer and a greater attention to the power relations embedded in literacy practices. With regard to current debates about the nature of literacy campaigns, I argue against the 'mass' campaign favoured in many Agency circles and in favour of rooting campaign work in local cultures and local definitions of 'need'. Recent developments in the ethnography of literacy suggest a far richer picture and a more complex framework for planning than previous campaign organizers have envisaged.

1 Putting Literacies on the Political Agenda

1990 was International Literacy Year. According to the Task Force set up to co-ordinate activities around the world, the main objective was to create public awareness and 'develop an atmosphere of positive attitudes towards the problem of illiteracy as a cultural problem and the need to tackle and combat it'. Worthy sentiments, but do they reveal serious flaws in the way that literacy is treated in public discussion? Do problems in the construction of literacy and 'illiteracy' themselves lie at the root of many of the 'problems' ILY was supposed to address? In their coverage of literacy issues, whether in the Third World or in the UK, both politicians and the press have a few simple stories to tell that deflect attention from the complexity and real political difficulties these issues raise. Attention is frequently restricted to scare stories on the numbers of 'illiterates' both in the Third World and within 'advanced' societies; patronizing assumptions about what it means to have difficulties with reading and writing in contemporary society; and the raising of false hopes about what the acquisition of literacy means for job prospects, social mobility and personal achievement.

Campaigners as well as agencies and governments still make great play of figures that show, say, 25 per cent of the UK to be 'illiterate', or 25 million people in the USA; a reflex in assessing the degree of 'development' in Third World countries remains their literacy 'rate'; and United Nations' statements highlight the increasing absolute numbers of 'illiterates' in the world, while calling meaninglessly for the 'eradication of illiteracy by the year 2000'. The figures are, of course, counters in a political game over resources: if campaigners can inflate the figures then the public will be shocked and funds will be forthcoming from embarrassed governments, or Aid Agencies can be persuaded to resource a literacy campaign.

The reality is more complex, is harder to face politically, and requires qualitative rather than quantitative analysis. Recent studies have shown, for instance, that when it comes to job acquisition the level of literacy is less important than issues of class, gender and ethnicity: lack of literacy is more likely to be a symptom of poverty and deprivation than a cause (Graff, 1979). Researchers (cf. Levine, 1986) also point out that the literacy tests which firms develop for prospective employees may have nothing to do with the literacy skills required on the job: their function is to screen out certain social groups and types, not to determine whether the level of literacy skill matches that of the tasks required. Some employers, for instance, have the somewhat mythical belief that employees who have learnt literacy are less likely to be antagonistic to new technology, computers, etc., and use literacy tests as a screen for these supposed attitudinal qualities. While some individuals find that attendance on literacy programmes does lead to jobs they would not have got otherwise, the number of jobs in a country does not necessarily increase with literacy rates, so in many cases other people are simply being pushed out – those with literacy difficulties may be leap-frogging each other for scarce jobs. Governments have a tendency to blame the victims at a time of high unemployment and 'illiteracy' is one convenient way of shifting debate away from the lack of jobs and onto people's own supposed lack of fitness for work. But many tasks require minimal literacy or a different kind of literacy skill than is taught at school, and employers can sometimes teach these on the job fairly easily: lack of literacy skills is not so frequently a real barrier to employment as the public accounts suggests.

Lack of literacy skills may also be less of a handicap in daily life than is often represented. The media likes to tell heroic stories of the 'management' of illiteracy, how 'illiterates' get around the city or bypass written exercises like form-filling or reading labels.

The situation, however, need not be represented as though people are suffering from some disease or handicap. Fingeret (1983), for instance, has shown how communities develop networks of exchange and interdependence in which literacy is just one skill among many being bartered: a mechanic without literacy skills may exchange his skills in car maintenance for a neighbour's ability to fill in a form; a businessman may speak a letter into a tape for a friend to write up, much as medieval monarchs used scribes. In this situation the acquisition of literacy skills is not a first order priority at the individual level, so long as it is available at the community level. Many immigrant groups have found themselves in similar situations, with 'gatekeepers' learning specific literacy skills relevant to their particular situation and often mediating with agencies of the host community. Among the Hmong of Philadelphia, for instance, sensitive literacy teachers have abandoned traditional, exam-oriented literacy teaching in favour of helping particular women develop sufficient commercial literacy to enable them to market their weaving and create an independent economic base (Weinstein-Shr, 1993; Weinstein-Shr and Quintero, 1994).

Such examples have led researchers and practitioners to talk of 'literacies' rather than of a single, monolithic 'Literacy'. It is not only meaningless intellectually to talk of 'the illiterate', it is also socially and cultural damaging. In many cases it has been found that people who have come forward to literacy programmes because they think of themselves as 'illiterate' have considerable literacy skill but may be needing help in a specific area. This could be treated as no different from any potential students applying to educational institutions, whether adult education or university postgraduate work. When applying to a literacy programme, adults who have defined themselves as 'illiterate' are often asked to read some written material so that their level and needs can be assessed: in one study in the USA they were asked to read texts produced by adult literacy students on the programme rather than 'top-down' published material and many found, to their own surprise, that they could read them fairly easily. Some, indeed, continued to read whole student magazines and publications, ignoring the 'test' aspect of the situation. Familiarity with content and context affected what were thought of as context-free, neutral skills in literacy decoding. While doing research among adult literacy students at a literacy centre in the UK, students told me of their concern that they could not learn literacy properly because they 'could not speak properly': that is, their dialect or pronunciation differed from Standard English. The *stigma* of 'illiteracy' is a greater burden than the actual literacy problems evident in such cases.

In many developing countries this stigma is still in the process of being constructed. People who have been accustomed to managing their daily lives, intellectual and emotional as well as practical and economic, through oral means have not required the elaborate definitions and distinctions associated with literacy and illiteracy in the West. In fact there are very few cultures today in which there is not some knowledge of literacy: children, for instance, learn to interpret logos on commercial goods and advertizements, or to 'read' television with its often sophisticated mix of script, pictures and oral language. Islamic societies have long been used to forms of reading and writing associated with religious texts and with scholarly and commercial activities, while in other contexts people have developed their own 'indigenous' writing system, used perhaps for specific purposes such as letter writing, sermons, or love notes. Literacy campaigns, however, have generally ignored these local literacies and assumed that the recipients are 'illiterate', beginning from scratch. Even Paulo Freire (1985) the most influential radical literacy campaigner, has tended to believe that people without western-type literacy are unable to 'read the world': his crusade to raise consciousness through literacy campaigns has been a leading challenge to dominant, authoritarian campaigns run by governments to do precisely the opposite, but it often rests on similar assumptions about the ignorance and lack of self-awareness or critical consciousness of 'non-literate' people. Recent research (Kulick and Stroud, 1993; Bloch, 1993) on the 'reception' of western literacies in various parts of the Third World has attempted to shift the focus from the 'impact' of literacy to the ways in which people 'take hold' of a particular literacy: this stresses the active rather than passive character of the recipients. Frequently, it has been recognized, people absorb literacy practices into their own oral conventions, rather than simply mimic what has been brought. Where, for instance, there were rules in oral communication about not thrusting oneself forward, not offending others, but still getting your own way through subtle self-effacing uses of language, then the introduction of writing often leads to similar conventions being used for letters, political documents or love notes. Similarly, linguistic and political self-awareness is often expressed through subtle forms of speech making and oratory in which participants express the difference between the surface message and inner meaning in various coded ways. Again this often passes over into the communicative repertoire introduced by the literacy campaign. To judge by the kinds of texts and writing introduced by some literacy campaigns, it might appear that the recipients have a better sense of this than the campaigners themselves: far from being passive and backward illiterates grateful for the enlightenment brought by western literacy, indigenous peoples have their own literacies, their own language skills and conventions and their own ways of making sense of the new literacies being purveyed by the agencies, the missionaries and the national governments.

It is evidence such as this that has led both researchers and those involved on the ground in teaching of literacy programme to revise the basic assumptions on which much literacy work has been conducted. The main shift that still needs to be addressed in the public debates that were stimulated by International Literacy Year involves the rejection of 'great divide' theory. According to this theory, to which I will be referring at various points in the book (see especially chapter 8), 'illiterates' are fundamentally different from literates. For individuals this is taken to mean that ways of thinking, cognitive abilities, facility in logic, abstraction and higher order mental operations are all integrally related to the achievement of literacy: the corollary is that 'illiterates' are presumed to lack all of these qualities, to be able to think less abstractly, to be more embedded, less critical, less able to reflect upon the nature of the language they use or the sources of their political oppression. It appears obvious, then, that 'illiterates' should be made literate in order to give them all of these characteristics and to 'free' them from the oppression and 'ignorance' associated with their lack of literacy skills. At the social level, 'great divide' theory assumes that there is a difference of kind as well as degree between societies with mass literacy and those with only minority or elite literacy. For economic take-off, it is claimed, a 'threshold' of literacy is necessary for social progress: developing countries must therefore be brought up to this level (sometimes cited as 40 per cent literacy in a population) in order for them to participate in the benefits of modernization, progress, industrialization and participation in the world economic order. Similarly, it is assumed that social groups which lack literacy but live within a mostly literate country will be disadvantaged or 'backward' and that their 'illiteracy' is a major cause of this: give them literacy and they will achieve social mobility, economic and political equality and participation in the social order.

These ideas appear so obvious to common sense that it seems both foolhardy and perverse to challenge them. Yet work in the field of literacy studies during the late 1980s and early 1990s, of the kind cited below (Graff, 1979; Finnegan, 1988; Gee, 1990; Barton and Ivanic, 1991) will hopefully lead researchers and practitioners in literacy programmes to develop more complex theories of literacy that reject 'great divide' thinking. These new approaches have important implications for policy and practice in this field, as this book attempts to bring out, but they do not always get adequate attention in public discussions.

Many researchers investigating the cognitive consequences of literacy (Goody, 1987; Olson, Torrence and Hildyard, 1985) now recognize that what is often attributed to literacy *per se* is more often a consequence of the social conditions in which literacy is taught. Literacy needs to be distinguished from education in terms of its supposed 'consequences'. Some kinds of education (though by no means all) may well inculcate critical self-awareness and facility with abstract concepts of the kinds claimed for literacy, but this has less to do with the inherent characteristics of literacy than with the character of the programme. There is, as this book demonstrates, significant counter-evidence of literacy learning in a variety of contexts (cf. Scribner and Cole, 1981; Gough, 1968; Mercer, 1988; Street, 1993), in which logic and critical thought play little part: one cannot therefore theorize that literacy in itself is associated with these things. Conversely, anthropological evidence (Finnegan, 1988; Bledsoe and Robey, 1986; Bloch, 1993) demonstrates that self-reflection and critical thought are to be found in supposedly non-literate societies and contexts. One crucial variable, for instance, in child development is what psychologists refer to as 'meta-linguistic awareness', the degree of self-consciousness about language. Many educationalists and developers (Teale and Sulzby, 1987; Lerner, 1958) have assumed that the acquisition of literacy is a key factor in developing this awareness. Anthropologists and sociolinguists (Finnegan, 1988; Besnier, 1989), however, have questioned this and suggested that the focus on an autonomous model of literacy deflects attention away from more complex social variables. One such variable, for instance, may be the number of languages spoken in a region (cf. Finnegan, 1988 on the Limba of Sierra Leone). Where people are in contact with or themselves speak a variety of different languages, they are likely to have developed a language for talking about language, to be aware of the character of different kinds of speech (and writing) and of the subtlety of meanings in different contexts. Play on figures of speech, skill in rhetoric as well as ability to develop and appreciate different genres are all features of so-called oral societies. Anthropologists, such as Finnegan, who have worked in these contexts soon find that 'great divide' thinking is no help in understanding the complexity and subleties of issues such as meta-linguistic awareness, which nevertheless dominate much contemporary educational practice and thinking. Differences in individual cognitive skills, then, are more likely to stem from such differences in social and cultural experience than from the presence or absence of literacy.

Literacy itself, moreover, varies with social context. It is difficult to lay down a single objective criterion for a skill that is nevertheless widely represented as the key to individual and social progress. In medieval England, for instance, ability to read Latin earned the label 'literatus'; in later periods, the major test was ability to read a prayer; many academic studies until recently used the ability to sign a marriage register as an index both of individual literacy and of literacy rates in the whole society; in many developing countries the returns to international agencies for the nation's literacy rate rest on numbers of children completing the first three, or five, grades of schooling. In the UK, too, the goal posts have been shifting and what was considered adequate literacy at the turn of the century would merit the label 'illiterate' by 'great divide' standards today. Recognition of the variable and contested criteria used to define literacy and illiteracy is probably more widespread now and one of the aims of International Literacy Year was indeed to develop popular sensitivity to the contextual nature of literacy skills. But the implications of this for broad pronouncements on literacy rates, proportions of 'illiterates' in a population etc., have not always been recognized, and much of the work in that year and subsequently continued to reinforce the more traditional stereotypes.

Misconceptions about their own 'illiteracy', for instance, continue to debilitate many adults in situations where the stigma derives from a mistaken association of literacy difficulties with ignorance, mental backwardness and social incapacity. When it is discovered that many who are labelled in this way, whether by themselves or others, have in fact minor difficulties with spelling, decoding, sentence or paragraph structure (or simply non-standard pronunciation!), it seems remarkable that so much cultural and emotional weight could have been placed on them. One reason has been the prevalence of 'great divide' theory: if these difficulties are associated with the category 'illiteracy' and that category is associated with lack of cognitive functions, or with backwardness, then the stigma is inevitable. If, on the other hand, they are located in a theoretical framework that assumes there to be a variety of litera*cies* in different contexts, no one line between literate and illiterate, and a range of cognitive and social skills associated with orality and literacy equally, then the agenda shifts and the stigma becomes meaningless. Everyone in society has some literacy difficulties in some contexts. (The classic 'middle class' difficulty is with income tax forms, but in this context the emotional charge is drawn off through humour and jokes rather than reinforced through categorical labelling and stigma.)

Current theory, then, tells us that literacy in itself does not promote cognitive advance, social mobility or progress: literacy practices are specific to the political and ideological context and their consequences vary situationally. This does not lead us to abandon attempts to spread and develop the uses and meanings of literacy: it does force us to question whether the current framework in which such activities are conducted is the most fruitful. The political task is then a more complex one: to develop strategies for literacy programmes that address the complex variety of literacy needs evident in contemporary society. This requires the policy makers and the public discourses on literacy to take greater account of people's present skills and own perceptions; to reject the dominant belief in uni-directional progress towards western models of language use and of literacy; and to focus upon the ideological and context-specific character of different literacies. International Literacy work should be used to help open up this debate and establish clearer concepts and frameworks on which practice can be based, not to reiterate worn clichés and patronizing stories about 'illiteracy'.

References

Barton, D. and Ivanic, R. (eds) (1991) *Writing in the Community*. Sage: London.

Baynham, M. (1993) 'Code Switching and Mode Switching: Community Interpreters and Mediators of Literacy', in B. Street (ed.) *Cross-Cultural Approaches to Literacy*. CUP: Cambridge.

Besnier, L.N. (1989) 'Literacy and Feelings: The Encoding of Affect in Nukulaelae Letters', *Text*, vol. 9, no. 1: 69–92.

Besnier, N. (1990) 'Literacy and the Notion of Person on Nukulaelae Atoll', *American Anthropologist*, no. 93.

Bledsoe, C. and Robey, K. (1986) 'Arabic Literacy and Secrecy among the Mende of Sierra Leone', *Man*, n.s., vol. 21, no. 2: 202–26.

Bloch, M. (1993) 'The Uses of Schooling and Literacy in a Zafimaniry

Village', in B. Street, (ed.) *Cross-Cultural Approaches to Literacy*. CUP: Cambridge.

Camitta, M. (1993) 'Vernacular Writing: Varieties of Literacy among Philadelphia High School Students', in B. Street (ed.) *Cross-Cultural Approaches to Literacy*. CUP: Cambridge.

Cook-Gumperz, J. (1986). *The Social Construction of Literacy*. CUP: Cambridge.

Dombey, H. (1988) 'Moving into Literacy in the Early Years of School', in J. McCaffery and B. Street (eds) *Literacy Research in the UK: Adult and School Perspectives*. RaPAL: Lancaster.

Fingeret, A. (1983) 'Social Network: a New Perspective on Independence and Illiterate Adults', *Adult Education Quarterly*, vol. 33, no. 3: 133–46.

Finnegan, R. (1973) 'Literacy Versus Non-Literacy: The Great Divide', in R. Finnegan and B. Horton (eds) *Modes Of Thought*. OUP: London.

Finnegan, R. (1988) *Literacy And Orality*. Blackwell: Oxford.

Gee, J. (1990) *Social Linguistics And Literacies: Ideology In Discourses*. Falmer Press: Brighton.

Goody, J. (1987) *The Interface Between the Written and the Oral*. CUP: Cambridge.

Gough, K. (1968) 'Implication of Literacy in Traditional China and India', in J. Goody (ed.) *Literacy in Traditional Societies*. CUP: Cambridge.

Graff, H. (1979) *The Literacy Myth: Literacy and Social Structure in the 19th Century City*. Academic Press: London.

Graff, H. (1987) *The Legacies Of Literacy: Continuities and Contradictions in Western Culture and Society*. Indiana UP: Bloomington, Indiana.

Grant, A. (1986) 'Defining Literacy: Common Myths and Alternative Readings', *Australian Review of Applied Linguistics*, vol. 9, no. 2.

Heath, S.B. (1983) *Ways with Words*. CUP: Cambridge.

Hill, C. and Parry, K. (1988) *Reading Assessment: Autonomous and Pragmatic Models*. Columbia UP: New York.

Hunter, C. and Harman, D. (1979) *Adult Illiteracy in the United States*. McGraw Hill: New York.

King, L. (1994) *Roots of Identity: Language and Literacy in Mexico*. Stanford UP: Stanford.

Klassen, C. (1991) 'Bilingual Literacy: the Adult Immigrant's Account', in D. Barton and R. Ivanic (eds) *Writing in the Community*. Sage: London.

Kulick, D. and Stroud, C. (1993) 'Conceptions and Uses of Literacy in a Papua New Guinea Village', in B. Street (ed.) *Cross-Cultural Approaches to Literacy*. CUP: Cambridge.

Lerner, D. (1958) *The Passing of Traditional Society*. Glencoe Free Press: New York.

Levine, K. (1986). *The Social Context of Literacy*. Routledge & Kegan Paul: London.

Lewis, I. (1986), 'Literacy and Cultural Identity in the Horn of Africa: the Somali Case', In G. Baumann (ed.) *The Written Word*. Clarendon Press: Oxford.

Lytle, S. and Wolfe, M. (1987) 'Alternative Assessment Project', unpublished report. University of Pennsylvania: Pennsylvania.

Mercer, N. (ed.) (1988) *Language and Literacy from an Educational Perspective*, 2 vols. Open University Press: Milton Keynes.

Olson, D., Torrance, N. and Hildyard, A. (eds) (1985) *Literacy, Language and Learning: the Nature and Consequences of Reading and Writing*. CUP: Cambridge.

Schieffelin, B. and Gilmore, P. (eds) (1986) *The Acquisition of Literacy: Ethnographic Perspectives*. Ablex: Norwood, New Jersey.

Schousboe, K. and Larsen, M. (eds) (1989) *Literacy and Society*. Akademsig Forlag: Copenhagen.

Scribner, S. and Cole, M. (1981) *The Psychology of Literacy*. Harvard UP: Boston, Massachusetts.

Shuman, A. (1986) *Storytelling Rights: the Uses of Oral and Written Texts by Urban Adolescents*. CUP: Cambridge.

Street, B. (ed.) (1993) *Cross-Cultural Approaches to Literacy*. CUP: Cambridge.

Teale, W. and Sulzby, E. (1987) 'Literacy Acquisition in Early Childhood: the Roles of Access and Mediation in Storybook Reading', in D. Wagner (ed.) *The Future of Literacy in a Changing World*. Pergamon Press: Oxford.

Wagner, D. (1987) *The Future of Literacy in a Changing World*. Pergamon Press: Oxford.

Weinstein-Shr, G. (1993) 'Literacy and Social Process: a Community in Transition', in B. Street (ed.) *Cross-Cultural Approaches to Literacy*. CUP: Cambridge.

Literacy and the construction of gender

Horsman, J. (1989) 'From the Learner's Voice: Women's Experience of Il/ Literacy', in M. Taylor and J. Draper (eds) *Adult Literacy Perspectives*. Culture Concepts Inc.: Ontario.

Rockhill, K. (1987a) 'Gender, Language and the Politics of Literacy', *British Journal of the Sociology of Education*, vol. 8, no. 2.

Rockhill, K. (1987b) 'Literacy as Threat/Desire: Longing to be SOMEBODY', in J.S. Gaskell and A. McLaren (eds) *Women and Education: a Canadian Perspective*. Detselig: Calgary.

Sarswathi, L.S. and Ravindram, D.J. (1982) 'The Hidden Dreams: the New

Literates Speak', *Adult Education and Development*, no. 19, German Adult Education Association, Bonn.

Stromquist, N. (1990) 'Women and Illiteracy: the Interplay of Gender Subordination and Poverty', *Comparative Education Review*, vol. 34, no. 1: 95–111.

Stromquist, N. (1992) 'Women and Literacy: Promises and Constraints', in D. Wagner and L. Puchner (eds) *World Literacy in the Year 2000*. Annals of the American Academy of Political and Social Science. Sage: London.

Literacy and development

Berggren, C. and L. (1975) *The Literacy Process: Domestication or Liberation?*. Writers and Readers Publishers' Cooperative: London.

Bhola, H. (1984) *Campaigning for Literacy*. UNESCO: Paris.

Freire, P. (1972) *The Pedagogy of the Oppressed*. Penguin: London.

Freire, P. (1978) *Pedagogy In Process*. Seabury Press: New York.

Freire, P. (1985) *The Politics of Education: Culture, Power and Liberation*. Macmillan: London.

Freire, P. and Macedo, D. (1987) *Literacy: Reading the Word and the World*. Bergin & Garvey: Massachusetts.

German Adult Education Association (1988) 'Literacy', special issue of *Adult Education and Development*, no. 31. Bonn.

McLaren, P. (1988) 'Culture or Cannon? Critical Pedagogy and the Politics of Literacy', *Harvard Educational Review*, vol. 58, no. 2.

Roberts, J. and Akinsaya, S. (eds) (1976) *Schooling in the Cultural Context: Anthropological Studies of Education*. David McKay Co.: New York.

Sjostrom, M. and R. (1983) *How Do You Spell Development?*. Scandavian Institute of African Studies: Uppsala.

Smith, M. (1981) 'Approaches to Literacy Work: a Short Annotated Bibliography', in Reading Rural Development Centre: Bulletin: Reading.

Street, B. (1987) 'Literacy and Social Change: The Significance of Social Context in the Development of Literacy Programs', in D. Wagner (ed.) *The Future of Literacy in a Changing World*. Pergamon Press: Oxford.

Street, B. (1990) 'Literacy Publications through the 80s', in 'Literacy and Development', vol. 27 of AERDD Bulletin. University of Reading: Reading.

UNESCO (1976) *The Experimental World Literacy Program: a Critical Assessment*. UNESCO: Paris.

Wagner, D. (1989) 'Literacy Campaigns: Past, Present, and Future', *Comparative Educational Review*, vol. 33, no. 2.

Weinstein-Shr, G. and Quintero, B. (eds) (1994) *Immigrant Learners and Their Families*. NCLE: Washington.

2 Literacy and Social Change: The Significance of Social Context in the Development of Literacy Programmes

I. Introduction

Those concerned with the 'future of literacy' must ask themselves what are the consequences for social groups and for whole societies of acquiring literacy. We need first, however, to consider the framework within which such questions are asked. The questions that have mostly been asked by agencies attempting to introduce literacy to societies where it has not been widespread, have generally stemmed from emphasis on the technical problems of acquisition and how these can be overcome. Within the framework of the 'autonomous' model of literacy, the question for agencies and those conducting literacy campaigns becomes: how can people be taught to decode written signs, and, for example, avoid spelling problems? This approach assumes that the social consequences of literacy are given – greater opportunity for jobs, social mobility, fuller lives, etc. – and that what the agencies need to address is the question of how literacy is to be imparted. This, however, takes too much for granted regarding the social implications of the process of literacy acquisition: there are other questions that need to be addressed prior to the apparently technical ones, questions derived from an alternative, 'ideological' model of literacy. It is useful to explore some of the implications of these models, and of the questions which arise from them, for the 'future of literacy' and for the conduct of literacy campaigns.

An argument repeatedly brought out in this book is that the 'autonomous' model is dominant in UNESCO and other agencies concerned with literacy. It tends to be based on the 'essay-text' form of literacy, dominant in certain western and academic circles, and to generalize broadly from this narrow, culture-specific practice. The model assumes a single direction in which literacy development can be traced, and associates it with 'progress', 'civilization', individual liberty, and social mobility. It isolates literacy as an independent variable and then claims to be able to study its consequences. These consequences are classically represented in terms of economic 'take-off' or in terms of cognitive skills. An 'ideological' model, on the other hand, forces one to be more wary of grand generalizations and cherished assumptions about literacy 'in itself'. Those who subscribe to this second model concentrate on the specific social practices of reading and writing. They recognize the ideological and therefore culturally embedded nature of such practices. The model stresses the significance of the socialization process in the construction of the meaning of literacy for participants, and is therefore concerned with the general social institutions through which this process takes place and not just the specific 'educational' ones. It distinguishes claims for the consequences of literacy from its real significance for social groups. It treats sceptically claims by western liberal educators for the 'openness', 'rationality' and critical awareness of what they teach, and investigates the role of such teaching in social control and the hegemony of a ruling class. It concentrates on the overlap and interaction of oral and literate modes rather than stressing a 'great divide'. The investigation of literacy practices from this perspective necessarily entails an ethnographic approach, which provides closely detailed accounts of the whole cultural context in which those practices have meaning. Until there are far more such accounts available one should be wary of making any generalizations about literacy as such.

II. The transmission of literacy

These models may be tested more directly against the immediate practical questions that are raised by consideration of comparative material from industrialized and developing nations and the questions raised by literacy campaigns, conducted both within and across nation-states. There are a number of ways in which the acquisition of literacy affects a society. For social groups with virtually no prior exposure to literacy it is likely that the dominant feature of acquisition will be not so much the consequence of literacy *per se* but the impact of the culture on the bearers of that literacy. By definition, literacy is being transferred from a different culture, so that those receiving it will be more conscious of the nature and power of that culture than of the mere technical aspects of reading and writing. Very often this process has involved some transfer of 'western' values to a non-western society. This aspect of literacy acquisition can be called, for convenience, 'colonial' literacy, and this chapter considers some contemporary examples of this, as well as citing some historical ones for comparison.

It is not always the case, however, that literacy is transferred from an alien society to indigenous 'illiterates'. In many situations it is a dominant group within a society that is responsible for spreading literacy to other members of that society and to subcultures within it. This has been the paradigm in many European cases of literacy transmission, as in France and Britain where bourgeois groups justified the expense of providing widespread literacy in terms of the spread of certain dominant class values (cf. Donald, 1981; Furet and Ozouf, 1984). The 'technical' advantages in terms of manpower skills, and so forth, were encapsulated within these values. In order to distinguish it from 'colonial literacy', this second kind of literacy transfer can be termed 'dominant' literacy and this chapter considers some examples in contemporary literacy campaigns, with particular reference to the author's own anthropological field-work in Iran during the 1970s.

A. 'Colonial' literacy

1. *Medieval England*

In order to bring out the ways in which the acquisition of literacy has to do with deeper aspects of ideology, culture and even epistemology (cf. Munasinghe, 1985), rather than just being an empirical matter of extending 'skills' and 'knowledge', it may be helpful to begin with an instance well removed in time from the present and thus, perhaps, less charged than many contemporary examples. Clanchy (1979), in his description of how the Normans introduced literacy in medieval England, argues that what was required was a shift to a 'literate mentality'. By this he means to indicate that the shift involves a way of thinking, a whole cultural outlook, an ideology, rather than simply a change in technical processes. Members of the culture, at least at certain levels of the hierarchy, came to share new assumptions about the status of the written word and its significance for claims about truth. In the eleventh century, rights to land and claims to truth were validated through, for instance, the display of swords and other such symbols of authority, through use of seals and through the oral testimony of a jury. By the fourteenth century certain classes of people, such as knights and local gentry, were referring, as a matter of course, to literate material such as 'pipe rolls', documents validated by a notary or letters that were dated precisely. A shift of this kind did not happen simply: it involved profound changes in people's sense of identity and in what they took to be the basis of knowledge. For instance, the spread of commercial documentation required the development of a system of dating. When a businessman wrote a letter he had to learn to put the date on it, for a number of reasons – in order to establish a basis for a sequence of further correspondence, in order to enable the letter to be retrieved easily later, and also so that the truth of the claims made in it could be tested against other evidence from the time. The dating of a letter, then, was not just a 'technical' matter but had legal and practical significance.

Moreover, during this era, development of the new convention of dating impinged upon deeply held religious beliefs. In medieval England the conceptual basis for the division of time was provided by Christian theology. Dating a document placed its maker in temporal and geographical perspective: it involved expressing an opinion about the writer's place in the world. The birth of Christ was the central reference point for current dating but this was a sacramental matter and not one to be lightly applied to temporal or commercial matters. The writer of a commercial document could not, then, simply date it with reference to the Christian calendar without giving possible offence both to the clergy and to the writer's own deeply held beliefs. Clanchy describes how a compromise developed, whereby secular dating was organized with reference to such events as the crowning of a king, while the religious calendar remained independent of commercial practice. The boundaries between the sacred and the profane were kept distinct within the new literate practices which were thereby accommodated to the belief system of the society into which they were being introduced. Clanchy, indeed, argues that the new 'mentality' became accepted precisely because it happened in such gradual ways, and did not therefore represent a great shock to traditional beliefs, even though over time the cumulative effect was quite radical. There is a lesson here for contemporary literacy agencies, in judging how far to take account of local perceptions and how far to simply impose their own 'outside' view of literacy.

Clanchy also describes how the very form of written texts is associated with deeply held beliefs, and how the transition from one system to another was achieved in Norman times by the 'mixing' of elements of the new and the old. What had given written texts legitimacy in the pre-Norman period had been their association with Christian truth. A Bible was a sacred object not only because of the content of the words on the page, but also in its material form and context. Certain Bibles, highly illuminated and preserved in monasteries, were held in esteem as reflections of the glory of God, the elaborate artwork cherished not simply on aesthetic grounds but as proof of the Beauty and Goodness of the Creator. When commercial documents began to circulate in greater numbers, there was some ambivalence, during the period of transition, as to how far they required embellishment and illumination as marks of the truth value of their content. Later, commercial and legal users of documents hence took to embellishing their writing, in order to try to acquire some of that status, and as a means to easing the transition from previous custom to new practices. Some of this has carried over into contemporary England in the way in which some legal and constitutional manuscripts are illuminated, the embellishments signifying their status and often having as much formal importance as the words on the page. Recognizing the problems associated with claiming validity for their assertions, politicians and others play upon the variety of ways in which different media of communication are taken to signify the truth.

In other parts of the contemporary world, too, the introduction or

spread of literacy practices is associated with theological and epistemological problems of the kind cited by Clanchy. Researchers and
agencies need to ask questions that would elicit similar information
about the compromises or breakdown that these problems may lead
to, and to find ways of describing and analyzing this level of the
literacy process across different cultures. Clanchy's work, in a sense,
provides a useful model for this endeavour, even though the conditions of medieval England are obviously very different from those of
the modern world. Both the way in which he approaches the material,
in terms of the concept of a 'literate mentality', and some of the
examples themselves, have general applicability. An analysis of one
or two more recent examples will bring this point out more fully.
These examples owe much to the 'ethnographic' approach to literacy
exemplified in Section 4 of this book, whereby literacy practices are
described as part of social wholes, in a way traditionally developed
by social and cultural anthropologists. These methods, and the
material they generate, suggest important questions and levels of
understanding that can usefully be applied to both the reserach and
the practice involved in contemporary literacy campaigns.

2. *Malagasy*

Maurice Bloch (1989) uses a combination of contemporary anthropological field-work and analysis of historical documents in order to
explain the sudden growth of historical manuscripts in Madagascar
in the nineteenth century. In doing so he brings out some general
aspects of the development of literacy in colonial contexts, that has
relevance to the contemporary situation and the current discussion.

   As in many non-European societies in this period, missionaries
were the first to contribute to mass literacy in Madagascar (cf.
chapter 7 below, where I discuss Clammer's (1976) account of
nineteenth-century Fiji, where missionaries took printing presses
with them to the island and taught only reading, not writing,
allowing the Fijians access only to the religious texts printed on the
presses). Roman script and printing were introduced to Madagascar
by the London Missionary Society from the 1820s, supplanting
Arabic which had been used for astrological and administrative
purposes. The missionaries translated the Bible and wrote it down in

Malagasy. At first the new literacy continued to be used mainly for administration, as well as for religious purposes. But from 1835 onwards the political situation changed dramatically. The London Missionary Society was expelled, Christianity was banned, the spread of literacy was seriously restricted and the schools closed. Yet both Christianity and literacy flourished in this period, which was one of the most productive for Malagasy literature. While administrative uses of literacy continued, the main development was in the production of historical and ethnographic manuscripts, many of which have survived until today.

Bloch explains these developments partly with reference to the knowledge he himself acquired during field-work on the island in the 1960s, among a group called the Merina. In Merina culture, knowledge was validated through being passed on from one generation to another. Elders passed on knowledge to their juniors and at the same time affirmed their political authority over those to whom it was being transmitted. The status of the elders was multi-faceted, and their authority depended upon a variety of social conventions: display of knowledge alone would be irrevant or ridiculous, but in the context of the power structure it represented a claim to power. The missionaries, with their 'Bible', were seen as making claims regarding their own authority, similar to those which Malagasy elders were accustomed to make through indigenous genealogies and stories. The Bible was seen as similarly consisting of accounts of the history and customs of the missionaries' ancestors, together with their genealogies, as indeed it does, and the accounts appeared, therefore, to be challenging those of the Merina themselves.

By asserting this knowledge the missionaries were seen to be overtly claiming a high place in the power structure and subordinating local authorities. As in Clanchy's example from medieval England, the significance of new forms of documentation lay in their location in a power structure rather than in the intrinsic qualities of the medium itself. Indeed, Bloch stresses that the significance of the written medium of communication lay not 'in the fact that it represented a different kind of knowledge to the oral knowledge of elders, but because it represented a more powerful, impressive, efficient form of the same kind of knowledge. A new technology had been harnessed for an old purpose to make a competing claim' (p. 11). The Merina, then, responded to the missionaries' Bible by writing their own 'Bible', with their own histories and genealogies and accounts of important legitimating events. This was what the Christian Bible consisted of, and it had likewise been part of the oral tradition in Malagasy. The adoption of written forms represented a continuation of traditional oral practice in the medium of literacy, a way of fighting back against the newcomers with their own weapons.

As in many responses to outside domination, the Merina pragmatically adopted aspects of the alien culture to their own conventions, while rejecting the Europeans' implied position of superiority in the power structure. As Bloch states: 'They used writing in this way, principally for administrative purposes, but also for ideological purposes. They therefore used writing in their reassertion of their history and customs against the political threat of outside predators, in the old way for these purposes' (p. 12). The written word, like oral knowledge, was carefully transmitted from authoritative person to authoritative person:

> What the Malagasy did in 19th century Madagascar with literacy was to use it as a tool for a kind of ideological practice which they had done before, orally ... Literary knowledge did not act on its own, rather people used literacy for their own purposes. The people who were using literacy were part of a system of social relations and therefore it was in terms of that system of social relations that literacy was significant and its relation to knowledge was in terms of these uses. Literacy did not desocialise knowledge, as implied by Goody. (Bloch, 1989, p. 12.)

Goody (1968) has argued that the advent of literacy creates a new distinction, between myth and history where 'history' refers to 'true' accounts of the past, unsullied by the particular social interests of those recording it. What the Malagasy example shows is that myth and history are both embedded within particular social conventions, and they do not necessarily correlate directly either with a distinction between truth and falsity or with that between orality and literacy. Both Christian uses of the text of the Bible and Malagasy uses of their own manuscripts served to maintain social conventions related to the assertion of power and the validation of knowledge. The ways in which myths are employed to validate present political positions does not necessarily change when they are written down. They do not automatically become altered or subjected to historical scholarship, for instance. The Malagasy could easily accommodate literate forms of communication, without the meaning or functions of the texts being radically changed. The development of literacy in itself did not alter the traditional bases of knowledge. Whereas Goody – and many development agencies – have assumed that the acquisition of literacy leads to a new kind of knowledge, more 'objective' and related to historical truth rather than myth, the evidence from ethnographic research suggests a more complex picture. As Bloch says: 'There is no such thing as non-social knowledge, whether literate or not' (p. 13).

The situations in Malagasy and in medieval England can both be taken as examples of 'colonial' literacy. Members of an outside culture introduced their particular form of literacy to a colonized people as part of a much wider process of domination. In both cases the introduction of certain literacy practices is to be understood in terms of that wider domination: in Malagasy, as part of the missionaries' attempt to spread their own religion and of the colonial administration to set up bureaucratic structures through which they could rule. In medieval England, the Normans introduced certain legal and bureaucratic forms of literacy in order to centralize their authority and to shift the basis for validating rights in land away from local sources. In both cases, however, we find something more than a simple imposition of dominant views on a passive indigenous population. Rather, local peoples find pragmatic ways of adopting elements of the new ideology, or of the new forms in which literacy is introduced, to indigenous belief and practice. In both cases, too, there was some degree of indigenous literacy prior to the colonial incursion, so that what was new was the particular forms which their uses of literacy took, rather than simply the presence of literacy itself.

B. 'Dominant' literacy

In most examples of colonialism one finds, similarly, that the subjugated peoples have had some acquaintance with literacy, notably in cases of Muslim groups and others with religions of the 'Book'. One would expect to find similar complex processes of adaptation, resistance and encapsulation when foreign forms of literacy are introduced in these contexts. This is also the case in countries not under direct colonial rule, but where some degree of indigenous differentiation of power and control means that the recipients of literacy campaigns are in practice experiencing 'foreign' cultural forms. In many cases the main agency of transmission today tends to be national governments and indigenous experts, frequently drawn from a narrow class or cultural base. On the one hand these situations frequently reproduce features of the 'colonial' situation, such as for instance in the employment of educators from western countries in local literacy campaigns. As participants at the Persepolis UNESCO Conference on Literacy (and the followers of Paulo Freire) have made clear, governments in the developing world and their internal agencies are often wedded to major features of western culture and style (Freire, 1978, 1985; UNESCO, 1975). Furthermore, at a structural level, these countries are often economically dependent on the western economic order, through multinationals, export dependency, loans and aid (Lloyd, 1971; Worsley, 1984). Very often, then, literacy is being introduced along with a whole range of features of western society – forms of industrialization, bureaucracy, formal schooling, medicine, and so forth.

On the other hand, beyond these obvious features of the 'colonial' model of literacy transmission, it is also important to take account of a degree of 'internal domination' in the ways in which literacy campaigns are being conducted. The primary dimensions of this new power structure involve hegemony of urban areas over rural, of men over women and of central elites over local populations. In order to understand the processes of literacy transmission in these contexts it is not enough simply to analyze the role of colonialism or of neo-colonialism; it is also necessary to develop ways of knowing about these local power structures and cultures.

Just as, in the overtly colonial situations described above for Malagasy and medieval England, there was local resistance and pragmatic adaptation to or modification of colonial literacy, so the contemporary situation of 'internal domination' is characterized by complex forms of adaptation to the new literacy practices being introduced. Again the model of literacy needs to be elaborated in order to make sense of this complexity and to understand what literacy means to the people acquiring it.

III. The case of Iran

An interesting, and perhaps extreme, example of 'internal domination' is to be found in many of the literacy campaigns conducted
under the Shah in Iran during the 1960s and 1970s. Many campaigns
were addressed to women as the main socializing agents and, in the
eyes of many, the major 'barriers to change'. In order to 'get at' the
children, it was believed, it was necessary to 'alter' their mothers.
One Iranian educationalist who played an important role in the
campaigns in Khorosan province suggested that, 'The psychological
attitudes of the Iranian villagers create a great obstacle to rural
reconstruction' (Gharib, 1966, p. 88). This psychological attitude, he
believed, stemmed largely from the influence of mothers. While the
father was considered to be an authoritarian head of the family, he
was usually out at work all day and it was the mother who passed
on values to the child. She, according to Gharib, was 'permissive',
had poor standards of health and hygiene and had a passive belief in
fate. As a result, Gharib states, 'Family life remains the most stubborn
core of resistance to change; [the home] contradicts the principles
taught at school [and it is necessary to educate] mothers as well as
daughters' (p. 88). Hashemi (1966) agrees that, 'It is in the home that
attitudes are fixed, ways of life established and traditions continued.
The profound change in patterns of behaviour and expectations
depends on a great part upon the attitude of the home-maker' (p.
98). The education of women, then, is central to education and
development: 'their education might be the way for removing remaining social, cultural and psychological barriers to the advancement of
a nation' (Hashemi, 1966, p. 107).

It was the role of the teacher in the village to make these changes
come about, in particular by challenging the conservatism of rural
women: 'The task of the teacher in rural areas is not so much that of
giving instruction in the classroom but of providing an integrated
education in social habits, agriculture techniques and the creation of
a new attitude of mind' (Gharib, 1966, p. 45). Teams of trained
women teachers could be drafted into villages to transform values.
Unfortunately, for the proponents of this scheme, women were
reluctant to move far from home to train as teachers. In 1964, when
Hashemi and Gharib were writing, only 9 per cent of rural teachers

were women and only 18 per cent of their pupils were girls. More-over, most teachers were reared and educated in cities and this, Gharib comments, made them 'usually unable to perform their task adequately', since their task was defined as becoming rural commu-nity leaders and transforming values. Gharib's solution was to set up Rural Teacher Training Colleges in local communities, so that rural people could be brought in, given some teaching experience and knowledge and then, before they became wedded to urban ideas and used their education to migrate, they would be sent back to the villages to teach fellow peasants.

From an educator's point of view Gharib's proposals had much merit, and were certainly an improvement on earlier authoritarian, urban-based practice that failed to recognize the importance of women in education. But, in a context where the national drive was towards rapid Westernization, and where most urban Iranians shared the views outlined above regarding 'backward' villagers, there was a crucial ambivalence in Gharib's proposals similar to that found in many such campaigns. The ambivalence lies on the one hand in the fact that, if the process was to be one of major indoctrination, changing fundamental beliefs and practices and the very bases of knowledge among the majority of the population, then a few rural teachers trained in rural areas and insulated to some extent from urban influences were not likely to have much impact. On the other hand, the introduction of urban teachers to rural areas was already creating resistance and resentment.

There was also a deep ambivalence among villagers towards the state education system and the forms of literacy it transmitted. They saw urban teachers as looking down on them, as interested in their own urban advancement rather than in educating villagers, and as failing to understand rural values and material needs, all of which was indeed true. Nevertheless, it tended to be assumed that one or two boys in each family would take advantage of the State education system, go on to higher levels of schooling and university in the city to obtain urban jobs. The main image of the new employment to which such education could lead was that it involved working at desks in clean, modern offices, with high salaries and security, in overt contrast with rural dependence on the vagaries of the climate and the general discomfort of working in the fields. So the urban teachers in the village found some village boys motivated to attend and learn. But the majority, it was assumed, would remain in the villages, work in the fields or orchards and support their ageing parents.

For girls the likelihood of continuing their education was even more remote. It was assumed that they would marry young, and that their major function was to rear children and look after the household. Each year a few girls would pass through to the top grades of the local village school and a decision would have to be made as to whether they could continue their education in urban schools. There were a number of factors to be taken into account. The family would need to have relatives whom they could trust in the town, or a house of their own, so that the girl had somewhere to live and someone to chaperone her while studying there. The parents would have to be committed to breaking tradition by allowing her to continue: the most likely job she could get would be as a teacher and, for many villagers, this was self-evidently a low-status occupation, given the low pay and poor standards of the teachers they encountered. There would also, of course, be problems in finding an appropriate husband.

All of this is familiar from many other parts of the world, but it indicates the importance of understanding local beliefs and values and local perceptions of literacy, rather than simply imposing them from outside. The effect of all of these factors, as regards both boys and girls, was a mixed and somewhat confused situation. Many boys who did 'succeed' in the education system found themselves without jobs of the kind their parents envisaged as the Iranian economy began to break down in the later part of the 1970s. In the village where I worked, in which ownership of orchards and sale of fruit provided a relatively lucrative source of income, educated boys might be better off returning to organize their plots in the village than hanging around disaffected and underemployed in the city. But their new literacy, and the aspirations developed through their urban education, did not prepare them for this kind of work. On the other hand, many who stayed in the village found that their education at the local *maktab*, or Qur'ānic school, prepared them better for the new, 'commercial' literacy required of village entrepreneurs than would the new State education. Moreover, these youths might finish up both wealthier and with more security than those trained in the 'modern' literacy of the State education system (cf. Street, 1984).

For girls too the picture was uneven. Some girls from the village did continue with their education in the city each year, and there were large numbers of women studying at the local university. Many village women with whom I spoke saw the advantages of schooling and literacy, and said that they would have liked it for themselves, and some older women did take advantage of the adult literacy classes that were being provided by central agencies. Women themselves had views on these matters, and were not simply the passive instruments of conservatism caricatured by outside, male educators.

Moreover, there was already a long tradition of forms of education and literacy in rural Iran, so that urban educators were not simply working on unsophisticated or 'uneducated' minds (cf. Arasteh, 1960). The villagers were already accustomed to the educational traditions imparted through the *maktab*s, and in many cases these were supplemented by local 'reading groups', in which people gathered at each others' homes to read *sūrah*s of the Qur'ān and passages from the commentaries, as a basis for discussion and interpretation. These processes provided the basis for village literacy well before western-style and state interventions. In the *maktab* the *mullāh* would provide basic knowledge of the Qur'ān, mostly through rote learning for younger pupils, although even here the process was not as one-dimensional and mindless as many western caricatures of it have suggested. At one level the students were learning many of the hidden conventions of literacy: the ordering of words on a page; the indicating of meaning by precise placing of words, whether in margins, as headings or across the main text at an angle; the indication of the beginning and ending of words by different forms of a letter.

In this sense, then, *maktab* students cannot be deemed 'illiterate', although they may well appear so in government and formal school tests designed to examine other, less 'hidden' skills. What students of the *maktab* acquired as part of their *maktab* literacy was not an obvious, or even a universal, aspect of literacy skills: it was a specific skill derived from the specific nature of the literacy materials they used, and of the context of learning in which they encountered them (cf. also Wagner, Messick and Spratt, 1986). Many of these aspects of literacy learning are not taught in modern, State schools, so one cannot simply equate village learning and literacy with 'backward' conservatism and modern schooling with 'progress' and critical thought, as many are wont to do. For instance, despite the stereotypes that associate Qur'ānic learning with mindless repetition, that imparted in the villages of Iran frequently involved some discussion and analysis, and did give scope for interpretation and criticism, particularly at higher stages.

The skills and processes developed within *maktab* literacy were, in terms of western pedagogy, 'hidden' rather than explicit, but they provided an important basis for some villagers to build on them a form of 'commercial' literacy that enabled them to cash in on the oil boom of the 1970s. With the help of this 'commercial' literacy they created an infrastructure for the production and distribution of village fruit to urban areas as demand increased. The *tajer*s or middlemen adapted their *maktab* literacy to these new requirements: this involved signing cheques, writing out bills, labelling boxes, listing customers and their deals in exercise books, recording fruit held in store, etc. In all of these transactions, use was being made of the 'hidden' literacy skills acquired within *maktab* literacy. These skills were being elaborated in new ways, and new conventions were being adopted specific to the expanded commercial enterprises. This involved, for instance, the attention to layout as a factor in constructing meaning that had been learnt through reading of the Qur'ān and the commentaries.

Local perceptions and uses of literacy, then, may differ from those of the dominant culture, and must be taken into account in order to understand the literacy experience of different peoples. All of this represents a different picture from that presented by those urban educators who see only 'ignorance' or 'backwardness' in the village. The over-emphasis, in Iran, on this urban perspective on literacy, meant that educators failed to identify those features of local literacy and culture most likely to facilitate adaptation to the new economic order of the country in the 1970s. Rather than seeking to impose a particular literacy and ideology on rural life, as the quotes above from Iranian educators suggest was the dominant viewpoint, observers might have looked at how the villagers themselves perceived the different literacies to which they were exposed and how they made pragmatic adaptations to serve their particular interests, in a similar way to the Malagasy situation. These examples also suggest that, in most cases in the contemporary world, literacy is not being introduced entirely fresh to 'illiterate' populations. Rather, most people have some experience of forms of literacy, whether as in these cases, through traditional religious texts, or as in many other circumstances, through exposure, however minimal, to the commercial literacy of local elites or neighbouring cultures. In all of the cases the reality is of a mix of oral and literate conventions, and the introduction of specific forms of literacy through education and agency campaigns represents a shift in those conventions rather than the introduction of an entirely new process.

IV. Conclusion

If one would like to anticipate some aspects of the 'future of literacy', ethnographic methods and theories about culture and change would need to be applied to the different literacies currently practised and experienced by people from different class and cultural backgrounds. This involves, in the first instance, developing respect for this variety rather than attempting to impose a single, uniform 'autonomous' model on local practice. The conflict between these two views of literacy has important implications for the conduct of literacy campaigns, and I shall conclude with a brief examination of some of the arguments conducted by a number of literacy specialists.

Some specialists, such as Heribert Hinzen of the German Adult Education Association, have argued that literacy planners should look more closely at 'research being done by anthropologists on the variety of literacy practices in different cultures and the relationship between literacy and education development' (Hinzen, 1984). He urges that education and literacy campaigns be rooted in and developed from these cultures themselves, rather than simply being imposed in terms of the cultural values of the campaigners themselves.

This view is challenged by H.S. Bhola, who characterizes Hinzen's approach as 'cultural relativism' and he identifies within it a 'new paternalism'. It involves those already educated and literate in 'telling the Third World that their illiterates are not ignorant but wise; that being illiterate can be dignified in its own peculiar way' (Bhola, 1984b, p. 3). Bhola sees this as an attempt to 'freeze' indigenous values and techniques at the expense of teaching 'new communication skills brought to us by literacy' (p. 3). Bhola's perspective is, however, itself patronizing to many 'Third World' societies, since it ignores the communication skills and forms of literacy that already exist there, as was evident from the examples of Malagasy and Iran cited above. What the ethnographic evidence suggests is that the major change brought by literacy campaigns is not simply in the introduc-tion of new communication skills but in the particular, often western-oriented forms of literacy and of ideology being imparted, and in the altering of the previous 'mix' of orality and literacy in the receiving culture.

It is not, as Bhola's approach might lead us to believe, a simple choice between 'freezing' traditional values on the one hand or of crude 'modernism' on the other. Rather the issue is that of sensitivity to indigenous cultures and recognition of the dynamic process of their interaction with dominant cultures and literacies. The reality, in such situations, is of pragmatic adaptation, particularly on the part of the less powerful party, to the new skills, conventions and ideologies being introduced. The particular 'literacy' being imparted through campaigns, whether conducted by national governments or by colonial powers, involves conventions and assumptions alien to those socialized into indigenous forms of literacy. The outcome is most often a mix of new and old convention: in reality, there is continuous interaction and change, and people frequently maintain a number of different literacies side by side, using them for different purposes, as Wagner and colleagues have discovered in Morocco (Wagner et al., 1986; Wagner, 1987) and Scribner and Cole in Liberia (1981). Indeed linguists, psychologists and anthropologists are just beginning to describe these processes in more sophisticated and less culturally biased ways (Wagner, 1983; Olson, Torrence and Hildyard, 1985; Heath, 1983; Bledsoe and Robey 1986; Street, 1988). Those involved in practical, literacy campaigns on the ground would do well to take advantage of this contemporary research, and to abandon outdated and ethnocentric models of literacy that can only distort practical efforts.

Some specialists still maintain that this kind of research is 'neither possible nor necessary in the policy-making world' (Bhola, 1984b, p. 3). Rather, they put their faith in the cultural ideals and literacy conventions of the dominant, usually western-oriented, classes in non-western countries and see the 'future of literacy' as being bound up with the strategic and practical problems of how their view of literacy can be spread to the masses. Bhola, for instance, argues that the only strategy commensurate with the size of the problem of illiteracy today is the national, mass-scale literacy campaign (Bhola, 1984a). Ethnographic research, however, suggests that local literacies are too substantial to be simply 'accommodated' to a single dominant 'autonomous' model. The complexity of the situation is disguised when literacy planners devise mass campaigns that treat local variation as something to be at best tolerated and, as in some of the cases cited above, denigrated.

Indeed, in some recent literacy campaigns, such as that in Nicaragua, planners and politicians have discovered for themselves that local experience cannot be simply 'accommodated' while it is assumed to be inferior, backward and a 'barrier to progress', and they have begun to pay explicit attention to local forms of literacy and culture as part of the very ideology of the campaign itself (see below, p. 138; Miller, 1985). They have provided a response to the advocates of the 'autonomous' model of literacy on the political level similar to that being developed here on a theoretical level: namely a recognition that literacy is part of ideological practice and will no more conform to the grand designs of central planners than will the members of the different cultures that happen to be defined within a given nation-state. Others would do well to follow their example. For the way in which 'local variations' are 'accommodated' to the hegemonic character of central campaigns will provide the fundamental question for those concerned with the 'future of literacy' in the next decades. Such questions can only be answered if we conduct more research into the varieties of literacy and forms of communication to be found in the contemporary world, in terms of the 'ideological' rather than the 'autonomous' model of literacy. In the field of literacy neither theory nor practice can be divorced from their ideological roots.

References

Arasteh, R. (1960) *Education and Tradition in Iran*. Brill: Leiden.

Asad, T. (1980) 'Anthropology and the Analysis of Ideology', *Man*, n.s., vol. 14, no. 4.

Bhola, H.S. (1984a) *Campaigning for Literacy*. UNESCO: Paris.

Bhola, H.S. (1984b) 'Letter to *Unesco Adult Information Notes*', no. 3.

Bledsoe, C. and Robey, K. (1986) 'Arabic Literacy and Secrecy among the Mende of Sierra Leone', *Man*, n.s., vol. 21, no. 2: 202–26.

Bloch, M. (1989) 'Literacy and Enlightenment', in K. Schousboe and M.T. Larsen (eds) *Literacy and Society*. Akademsig Forlag: Copenhagen.

Bourdieu, P. and Passeron, P. (1977) *Education and Cultural Reproduction*. Sage: London.

Centre for Contemporary Cultural Studies (1980) *Language, Culture, Media*. Hutchinson: London.

Clammer, J. (1976) *Literacy and Social Change: a Case Study of Fiji*. Brill: Leiden.

Clanchy, M. (1979) *From Memory to Written Record: England 1066–1307*. Edward Arnold: London.

Donald, J. (1981) Language, Literacy and Schooling, Open University course No. U203, *Popular Culture*.

Freeland, J. (1985) 'The Literacy Campaign on the Atlantic Coast of Nicaragua', *World University Service News*, nos 1 and 2.

Freire, P. (1978) *The Pedagogy of the Oppressed*. Seabury Press: New York.

Freire, P. (1985) *The Politics of Education: Culture, Power and Liberation*. Macmillan: London.

Furet, F. and Ozouf, J. (1984) *Reading and Writing: Literacy in France from Calvin to Jules Ferry*. CUP: Cambridge.

Gharib, G.S. (1966) 'Training Teachers for Rural Elementary Schools in Iran', MA Thesis, University of Beirut.

Goody, J. (1968) *Literacy in Traditional Societies*. CUP: Cambridge.

Goody, J. (1977) *The Domestication of the Savage Mind*. CUP: Cambridge.

Hashemi, M. (1966) 'Adult Education in Rural Iran: Problems and Prospects', MA Thesis, University of Beirut.

Heath, S.B. (1983) *Ways with Words*. CUP: Cambridge.

Hinzen, H. (1984) 'Letter to *Network Literacy*', vol. 1.

Lloyd, P. (1971) *Classes, Crises and Coups*. Granada: London.

Mace, J. (1979) *Working with Words*. Chameleon: London.

Miller, V. (1985) *Between Struggle and Hope: the Nicaraguan Literacy Crusade*. Westview Press: Boulder, Colorado.

Munasinghe, V. (1985) 'An Analysis of Some of the Social and Epistemological Implications of the Acquisition of Literacy', unpublished thesis. Anthropology and Linguistics Group: University of Sussex.

Olson, D., Torrence, N. and Hildyard, A. (eds) (1985) *Literacy, Language and Learning: the Nature and Consequences of Reading and Writing*. CUP: Cambridge.

Scribner, S. and Cole, M. (1981) *The Psychology of Literacy*. Harvard UP: Cambridge, Massachusetts.

Street, B.V. (1984) *Literacy in Theory and Practice*. CUP: Cambridge.

Street, B.V. (1988) 'Literacy Practices and Literacy Myths', in R. Saljo (ed.) *The Written World*. Springer Press: Berlin/New York.

UNESCO (1975) *Final Report for International Symposium for Literacy, Persepolis*. Iran.

Wagner, D. (1983) (ed.) 'Literacy and Ethnicity', *International Journal for the Sociology of Language*, no. 42. Mouton: New York.

Wagner, D. (ed.) (1987) *The Future of Literacy in a Changing World*. Pergamon Press: Oxford.

Wagner, D., Messick, B. and Spratt, J. (1986) 'Studying Literacy in Morocco', in B. Schieffelin and P. Gilmore (eds) *The Acquisition of Literacy: Ethnographic Perspectives*. Ablex: Norwood, New Jersey.

Worsley, P. (1984) *The Three Worlds*. Weidenfeld & Nicolson: London.

Section 2:

The Ethnography of Literacy

Introduction

This second Section provides specific ethnographic accounts of literacy practices, elaborating my own anthropological field-work in Iran that was briefly referred to in chapter 2 above, and providing a critical survey of some ethnographic accounts. At this point it is necessary to explain further what is meant by an ethnographic account of literacy. A number of disciplines in recent years have begun to employ ethnographic methods, developing beyond the particular meanings and uses of them assumed within the discipline of anthropology in which they originated. Anthropologists tend to see ethnography in terms of 'participant observation', involving detailed descriptions of small groups and of their social and cultural patterns. Classically, an ethnographer lived among the people for several years, learning the language and applying to the collection of data rigorous theory and method derived from previous experience of anthropologists in the field. Educationalists have taken over the term in recent years to refer to close, detailed accounts of classroom interactions, with perhaps some attention to the lives and roles of students outside the classroom setting. Sociolinguists often have in mind networks and immediate contexts of interaction between speakers when they use the term. In all of these cases, new accounts of literacy in practice are being generated to supplement, and in some cases supplant, those available previously through experimental methods. The call in the 1980s was for ethnographic descriptions of literacy and it was assumed that new generalizations could be built upon such accounts, once we had enough of them. However, the different meanings of the concept and the different implications of the methodology were often not explored in any depth: ethnography was considered a good thing and its results would be the basis for a more satisfactory 'knowledge' of literacy. In this Section I examine these assumptions in some detail, using my own anthropological field-workers in Iran. I consider, for instance, the implications of including in 'ethnography' written texts from the culture being studied, where field-workers had traditionally relied upon oral evidence. I analyse the problems implicit in some earlier anthropological accounts of literacy that may have used ethnographic method but which rested on what now appear flawed theoretical premises. Ethnography on its own is not a magic solution to the 'problem' of investigating literacy: without theoretical clarity the empirical investigation of literacy will only reproduce our own prejudices, whatever meaning we attach to 'ethnography'.

Chapter 3: The Uses of Literacy and Anthropology in Iran

I attempt to develop Richard Hoggart's seminal work, *The Uses of Literacy*, and to consider the implications of applying his methods to anthropological field-work in Iran. This requires some analysis of the different conceptions of 'culture' employed within cultural studies, as it emerged in the UK in the 1960s and 1970s and of the discipline of social anthropology, as it developed its distinct character in post-war Britain. I then apply some of these ideas to developments in rural education in Iran during the 1970s. Some of the text books used for educating villagers in Iran during the reign of Reza Pahlavi employed themes derived from Iranian oral tradition dating back not only to pre-Pahlavi times but to much earlier pre-Islamic periods. Different epistemologies underlay the accounts in the modern educational system and those in traditional folklore. Attempts were made by those who wrote the school text books to play upon the authority of these earlier accounts, while implicitly purveying a radically different view of science, truth and knowledge, and a patronizing and demeaning view of past thinking. This process was not, however, simply one-way, a dominant centre exerting hegemony over passive peoples in the villages: in practice the Shah's rather crude formulations were often revised in local thinking and assimilated to quite different epistemologies. This process of struggle over meanings in texts, of resistance to top-down educational strategies and of pragmatic adaptations to centralist hegemony reflect the material examined in other chapters of this book regarding the transfer of literacy and culture. In this context I am particularly concerned with methodological questions and specifically with the application of Hoggart's methods of studying literacy in northern England to the setting of village Iran. Ethnographers can no longer simply arrive in an 'isolated' village and study only local practice: ethnographers in the contemporary world, as they study local literacies, will require some knowledge of the central literary tradition in the country studied, including both folk traditions and the immediate cultural background of those who write the modern texts for village children. There is scope here for a fruitful combination of literary critical and anthropological approaches. I conclude with the hope that, on the basis of actual evidence of literacy in practice, built upon the theoretical and methodological approaches discussed here and throughout the book, new understandings of literacy and valid generalizations about it will be developed in the coming decade.

Chapter 4: Orality and Literacy as Ideological Constructions: Some Problems in Cross-cultural Studies

This chapter addresses the central irony that, while contemporary anthropology has provided one of the major stimuli for the new directions in literacy studies, towards culturally sensitive accounts of literacy in practice, some of the classic accounts of literacy in traditional society by anthropologists have been written from the perspective of the 'autonomous' model of literacy and tend therefore to reproduce technicist and acultural accounts of literacy. This argument is explored in relation to specific descriptions by anthropologists of the 'cargo cult' phenomenon. Best documented among native peoples in Melanesia before and after the Second World War, cargo cults developed as responses to western penetration, and as attempts to wrest the goods or 'cargo' away from the new arrivals – to re-assert local rights and local values. Anthropologists provided some of the first detailed accounts of these cults, attempting to explain them in terms of indigenous meanings rather than dismiss them as irrational superstition, as did many politicians and missionaries. Yet, when these same anthropologists approach the role of literacy in cargo cults they appear to abandon their relativist disciplinary training and experience and revert to accounts of indigenous 'irrationality', of 'ritualized' literacy and 'mistaken' thinking that they had eschewed when describing religious and other institutions. One explanation for this shift is that these anthropologists were employing, implicitly, an 'autonomous' model of literacy. One assumption of this model that is followed in the 'cargo cult' literature is that literacy is intrinsically associated with logic and rationality so that if local peoples use it for religious or ideological purposes they are somehow misunderstanding its nature. I argue on the contrary that the uses of literacy in cult practices and rituals represent an accurate understanding of the ways in which literacy was being employed by the colonists and missionaries. For they themselves constantly employed literacy for ideological and political rather than purely 'logical' and 'rational' purposes. As in Malagasy, Iran, India and the other sites of literacy practice described throughout the book, the uses and meanings of literacy in Melanesia involved some pragmatic adaptation of local concepts and ideals to the political and economic realities imposed by western colonists. Such ideologically and politically sensitive accounts of literacy practices were prevented by the framework imposed by an 'autonomous' model of literacy: the New Literacy Studies, then, hold out the prospect of revised readings of many past accounts of culture contact in which literacy was a significant factor and provide a basis from which new ethnographies may be produced that are important not only for the rationality debate but also for our understanding of ideologies of power.

3 The Uses of Literacy and Anthropology in Iran

This chapter is an attempt to apply some of the principles of Richard Hoggart's *The Uses of Literacy* (1957) to the understanding of literacy practices in Iranian villages, where I did anthropological field-work during the 1970s. Searching for a research literature to help make sense of the complexity of the local uses and meanings of literacy in Iran, I was concerned to find instead that the development and educational accounts of literacy at that time – rooted in an autonomous model of literacy – tended to provide accounts of village life that ignored or demeaned local literacy practices. Turning to the anthropological literature, which was still dominated by the work of Goody, whose *Literacy in Traditional Societies* (1968) I had with me in the field, I discovered that his theories of literacy simply reinforced notions of the 'great divide' between literacy and orality and deflected attention away from real literacy practices and their meanings for local lives. One set of literature which appeared to provide a more culturally sensitive and fine-tuned account of how people used literacy and what it meant to them in their everyday lives and social relations, was to be found however in the 'cultural studies' tradition, itself influenced by my discipline of anthropology but also more conscious of textual traditions and their social embeddedness. The work of Hoggart, Williams and others in this field, though located primarily in British working life, suggested insights and questions that may help illuminate the rich experience of literacy practices I was encountering in Iranian villages. This chapter represents one attempt to make that cross-cultural link and to consider whether some aspects of that British experience and critical tradition could be usefully applied in a very different cultural context but one where similar processes might be at work beneath the surface.

The Uses of Literacy was written in 1957 as an attempt to explore the effects of mass literacy in certain areas of life in England. Drawing upon personal memories of his boyhood in a working-class area of Leeds, Hoggart tries to round out a description of traditional life as a basis for analyzing certain changes, particularly those connected with mass literacy and the shifts in values that could be traced through it. He focuses on working-class concern with the home and the family, paying close attention to the phrases of daily speech, to details of clothing and furniture and housing and to attitudes that could be inferred from the style of life, from the ritual and formality, from the very tempo of conversation, from stance and gesture – all areas familiar to the anthropologist too. He deals with the sense of tradition, with what working-class people assume should be believed or done about certain matters. This involves attitudes to home, the mother, father and neighbourhood; such divisions of the world as that into 'us and them', and such notions as 'live and let live'; traditional emphases on the personal, concrete and immediate concern with such ideas as fate and luck and what he calls 'primary religion'; and aspects of taste that can be characterized by such terms as 'baroque'. He uses all of this as a basis for discussing and evaluating the kinds of changes brought about since the Second World War. He takes as a text for what becomes almost a sermon, De Toqueville's analysis of democracy in America: 'By this means, a kind of virtuous materialism may ultimately be established in the world, which would not corrupt, but may enervate the soul, and noiselessly unbend the springs of action' (quoted in Hoggart, 1957, p. 169).

It is this unbending of the springs of action with which he is primarily concerned, the debilitation of what he considers stronger values in traditional working-class life. He compares some of the old and new values, concentrating on the 'regrettable' aspects of change and notes how the success of the new is often tied to its identification with the old, a point that has no little relevance to the study of literacy in other parts of the world as we have seen. Certain aspects of traditional life are particularly vulnerable to the attacks of the mass publicists. The concern with the personal, or with a friendly homely manner, are easily played upon by the smart, educated salesman and become hollow replicas of what was once a genuine feeling. The older 'tolerance' becomes a thoughtless and irresponsible attachment to the catch word of 'freedom'. ''Aving a good time' while you could within dire economic conditions, becomes a sloppy hedonism in the new age, while a slick conformity grows out of the group sense of earlier times. All of these changes, he suggests, represent an appeal to self-indulgence, materialism and self-gratification. Thus what might once have been a genuine sense of tradition that provided some term of reference for daily action might become, under the pressures of the new publicists working through mass literacy, a self-conscious and flattering posture, with no reference to actual beliefs.

Hoggart analyzes these processes in particular detail as they relate to what he calls the 'group sense'. The older awareness of the importance and rightness of the group has become, he believes, a callow democratic egalitarianism, used by popular publicists and advertizers. It thus becomes a simple belief that the majority must be right, what Hoggart calls the 'cant of the common man'. The expression 'I'm as good as you' becomes 'You're no better than me', a refusal to accept any differentiation of value or ability; thus everything is scaled down to the 'little' man's vision. In literature this involves a necessary direct communication between writer and reader, with no complexity or explication. The rejection of pretensions to which more complex writing is subject becomes a rejection of any ideas at all; it is an exaltation of the ordinary. It is revealed especially in the popular press, by those journalists who pretend to be working-class, homely fellows who reject the pomposities and over-complexities of 'them' and reduce everything to ordinariness – the extraordinary is dealt with by stereotyping as odd (the absent-minded professor, the weird scientist, etc.) and is thus brought within the recognizable world of the ordinary.

Hoggart feels that this leads to a meaningless indifferentism – everything becomes as one, there are no standards, no order, only a shabby appeal to sincerity for its own sake as justifying any actions – ''is 'eart was in the right place, any road'. Thus the sense of tension in life disappears and with it a taste for challenge; mass entertainment enervates, over-excites and finally dulls taste. The growth of literacy, far from leading to a deepening of response to literature and that complexity in life with which worthwhile literature is concerned, has led to a debasement of feeling, a narrowing of response, a weakening of traditions that were once healthy and strong. He does not maintain that working-class people have necessarily succumbed to this influence but is merely concerned with pointing out the extent to which such possibilities are present in mass literacy.

Much of this argument is familiar to anyone brought up during the 1960s and 1970s in Britain since it formed the central concern of much of the liberal, humanities curriculum and of endless television and radio discussion programmes. It is also implicit in much of the critical literature of book and film reviews in so-called 'high-brow' liberal magazines and newspapers. The reason why such views have spread so widely and deeply through liberal education in Britain is that they belong to a longer and quite significant tradition, of which Hoggart's work is only a recent well-known example. It has been called the 'culture and society' tradition, after a book by Raymond Williams which came out soon after Hoggart's and which attempted to document such shifts in ideas from a less sanctimonious, more sociological and socialist perspective (Williams, 1958). What he and similar writers are interested in is the continual engagement, as they see it, between the literary imagination on the one hand and the growing industrial capital culture on the other, from the time of the industrial revolution. According to a later survey, 'what more than anything else distinguished these literary/critical studies at this time was their attention to "meaning": how separate texts/rituals/institutions interrelated in a "whole way of life". Like anthropology, the approach involved a commitment to "interpret cultural phenomena in terms of structural relationships or parts of a whole"' (CCCS, 1978, p. 128). In the English critical tradition this has its origins in nineteenth-century literature and social criticism, in the response of certain writers to industrial society and culture and in new kinds of critical consciousness which that response gave rise to. It can be traced through the works of Matthew Arnold, William Morris, T.S. Eliot and others, and took on a particular colouring in the work of Leavis and writers for *Scrutiny* from the 1930s to 1950s. In the 1950s it was taken up, in their different ways, by Hoggart and Williams who, in the sense outlined above, were moving in a similar direction to anthropology. According to the Centre for Contemporary Cultural Studies that was founded by Hoggart to further such work (and which has now taken a far more radical turn than its founder), they were charting profound historical and cultural transformations in British society in the 1950s. *The Uses of Literacy* was, according to publicity for the Centre:

> an attempt to 'read' intuitively the cultural meaning of that period in British society from the inside; to see especially how change was being lived through and lived out in the 'felt' experience of men and women in the society; and to define the impact of the new mass media and the

more contemporary modes of feeling which they expressed, on the cultural attitudes, sentiments, values and traditions of working class life and experience. (Publicity for CCCS, 1978, p. 19)

Williams tackled the situation by revaluing the intellectual and imaginative response to industrial capitalism of a long line of writers, critics, social critics and philosophers (Williams, 1958). He critically defined certain crucial terms such as class, industry, democracy, art and culture, defined both in the way of writing about them at the time and in the lived, collective experience of the whole society. In this sense he was adding an anthropological perspective to literary criticism just as Lienhardt and others were later to add a literary critical dimension to their anthropology (Lienhardt, 1980).

Reinforcing this link between the two disciplines via a particular interpretation of 'culture', the Centre defined the term as:

the lived experience, the consciousness of a whole society; that particular order, pattern, configuration of valued experience, expressed now in imaginative art of the highest order, now in the most popular and proverbial forms, in gesture and language, in myth and ideology, in modes of communication and in forms of social relationship and organisation. (Publicity for CCCS, 1978, p. 19)

Where anthropologists have traditionally studied mainly the 'popular and proverbial forms', they are now having to pay more attention to other modes of communication conventionally the province of other disciplines. This involves particular attention to literate forms as these increasingly penetrate the cultures the anthropologist studies. In developing this aspect of their enquiries anthropologists may find themselves drawing more and more upon the literary/critical tradition and the terms of reference outlined by writers such as Hoggart and Williams, as they attempt to make sense of indigenous literacies and literatures in different parts of the world. If the modern villager in the Third World is affected by central education systems and by books, then the anthropologist will have to both analyze those texts and also look to the critical tradition that underlies them. The anthropologists thus find themselves with much background reading to be done even when they are studying a society that is mostly non-literate and has only occasionally direct links with the larger literate community.

This is the case in attempting some anthropological analysis of village life in Iran. Some account must be taken of the central intellectual tradition on the one hand, to be able to analyze its relationship to village life and thought; and on the other, some analysis of the nature of literacy and of the impact of written material on the daily life of the villager. Hoggart's attempts to show how attitudes and significant concerns may be represented in the detail, tone and atmosphere of daily life, as a basis for showing their relationship to mass literacy, may be of some help in undertaking a similar task in another society. I shall describe briefly the growth of the modern education system in Iran and some of the ideas that lie behind its development and then relate this to the situation in villages where I did field-work during the early 1970s.

The growth of the modern, centralized education system in Iran effectively begins in the mid-nineteenth century with Amir Kabir, adviser to Nasr Al-Din Shah (cf. Arasteh, 1964). Amir Kabir, seeing the need for training centres especially adapted to produce government administrators to run the growing number of Ministries being based on European political models, set up a polytechnic school, Dar Al-Farun, in 1848. This school was followed quite soon by more institutions specifically adapted to the needs of government and bureaucracy and controlled by a ruling elite who, as Arasteh comments, 'used education to manipulate the masses'. Arasteh comments:

> The government's need for a bureaucratic administration directly brought about a system of higher education geared to the production of trained government personnel who lacked, however, research or professional aims. (Arasteh, 1964, p. 20)

The fact that higher education in Iran did not develop out of centres of learning with a tradition of academic research, as in much of Europe, but out of specific needs of government departments, was one of the major causes of the difficulties faced by educational theorists in the 1960s and 1970s when they tried to introduce ideas from the liberal European tradition into this more overtly functional system. After the setting up of a Constitutional Monarchy in 1916, education was further centralized and another level of complexity was introduced with the use of the French education system as the model. The French emphasis on assimilating facts in an encyclopaedic theory of learning meshed to some extent with the traditional concern for rote learning based on Qur'ānic recitation, so that students worked very hard to amass knowledge rather than to think or criticize, a feature of contemporary education in the Middle East analyzed in greater depth by Ahmed Al-Shahi (1980). During my period as a lecturer at the University of Mashad in 1970–1, I was frequently to observe students at examination times, pacing up and down, each under their own street light, memorizing from text books in keeping with this early pattern of education. Against this background the Shah attempted to institute major reforms in education during the 1960s and 1970s. He set out two major and often conflicting aims: one, to provide sufficient appropriately trained people to run the modern state, in the tradition of Amir Kabir's polytechnic; and the other, to increase 'participation' in the life and activities of the modern state through mass literacy and the introduction of liberal perspectives into at least some areas of the curriculum. The central Ministry of Education was to oversee a pyramidal structure, from primary schools, the main source of state education in rural areas, through various strands of secondary education, to technical and university institutions in the major cities. Villagers were seen as a pool of potential skill that could be upgraded through various stages of the pyramid to fit the functional needs of the modern economy, while the education of the majority, including those left behind in this process, would serve to overcome their traditional backwardness and resistance to the modern world (cf. Hashemi, 1966; Seddigh Gharib, 1966; Bharier, 1971; Pahlavi, 1960).

As an anthropologist my interest – not unlike that of the cultural studies approach – was in how this structure actually touched the lives of people 'on the ground', particularly in rural areas where I did field-work, and the ways in which the contradictions and problems generated at the macro level were enacted in terms of people's daily lives at the micro level. A major theme for many villagers, as I have developed more fully elsewhere (Street, 1975, 1984) was the contrast between the new state system of education and the traditional *maktab* in which a local *mullāh* taught their children the basics of Islam. (See above, chapter 2.)

Many of the men were critical of the new schools and compared them unfavourably with their own experience at the *maktab*, although they also recognized that if their children were to get jobs in the modern sector, to which many aspired, then they would have to attend the state school. One point of contrast for the older generation was that their orthography was more careful and precise than that of those youths taught at the modern primary school and they were very critical of the teachers there for their carelessness, a theme that replicates much of the experience in England as mass education developed. Teachers at the new school certainly gave less time and attention to actual handwriting and precise reading than in the *maktab*. They were asked, as in the *maktab*, to read aloud from the text book and to learn it by heart but, in many of the classes that I attended, they often got words wrong or skipped whole lines without correction, the other children paying scant attention. This was partly a matter of numbers in the class: the *mullāh* taught Persian reading and writing only to those sent along by their parents, whereas the government school was obliged to take everyone and, at least in the younger age range, did in fact accommodate a large proportion of village youth so that classes were overcrowded and unmanageable. But there was also a fundamental distinction between the teachers in the two schools. Any teacher in the state system who had qualified at a teacher training college or a university was not really interested in working in a village but was obliged to by the Ministry of Education for the first few years after training. Many did so grudgingly and saw promotion only in terms of urban advancement. However, some village youths, partly under pressure from their parents, did want to use the state schools as a stepping stone to similar advancement and so struggled through the lessons and the exams in order to pass on to the secondary school in Mashad. Some of these went on to universities in Iran or abroad and developed professional and relatively well-paid careers, although by the mid 1970s many were finding such employment difficult and became one of the disaffected groups that helped bring down the Shah.

For the ones who left, then, progress was seen as outwards not upwards within the village. But this still left the majority with an education apparently not geared to their needs. What, then, did those youths who remained behind get out of the system? In the village of Cheshmeh, where I lived for some time during the early 1970s, they learned to read and write more fluently, though often less accurately, than those of their parents who had gone to the *mullāh*'s school. Some of them were able to adapt this to the business of selling and buying fruit, which their parents had previously accomplished successfully through adaptation of their *maktab* literacy (see

Street, 1984; and above). This involved filling out lists of the different fruits, writing out bills, writing their names on the appropriate boxes to be sent to the city, occasionally writing a letter to their dealer in Tehran. They also wrote cheques frequently and dealt with the village branch of a national bank. The money for a new bath-house was paid by cheque and the organizer would carry a list of names and show the cheques around. In this way literacy was incorporated into the existing framework of communication and reciprocity. There were no newspapers sold in the village and I never saw one brought from the city; the only book in a home would be the Qur'ān and, sometimes, a Persian commentary on it. The school text books were soft-backed, programmed affairs, moving through a series of lessons at the same pace in all schools across the country in the way borrowed from the French system and graded from beginning to the final village classes before passing on to the secondary school. Each subject had its own book – 'Language', 'Customs', 'Science' – and every school in the country used the same books. The student had no contact, in school or out, with any other kinds of book than these and the religious ones; there was no reading of popular novels, magazines, comics, hard-back literature, etc. (although towards the end of my stay some urban-educated youths were returning for short visits with such literature which they touted as a sign of their progress). When an exercise had been dealt with in a text book, the pages might be ripped out and used to wrap food; there was no sense of these books as permanent objects to be read at leisure, or of a book as 'imaginative literature', as communication of ideas between author and reader. School text books anywhere tend to have a flatness about them, a uniformity that allows little scope for choice or idiosyncracy and which does not present itself as a genuine communication between writer and student. These particular books were, in fact, well produced, with clear interesting pictures and carefully graded and presented text, but when they were not supplemented by any other kind of book not written specifically for the classroom, then it was inevitable that they would reinforce the idea of writing and reading as narrow chores dissociated from everyday life and meaning.

In the critical terms used by Hoggart and the English 'culture and society' tradition, this process allowed no scope for introducing students to the creative potential of the written word, to challenge, scrutiny and criticism. Indeed, pupils in the new government schools may have had less access to these possibilities than had those who only attended the *mullāh*'s school before, or who had no formal education at all. For in those traditional contexts there was access to creative literature and some scope for questioning and relevance. In Iranian villages this was embodied in two strong lines of oral tradition. One stemmed from the religious life of the village and involved both repetition of *sū-rah*s of the Qur'ān and stories about the Prophet and his Companions that allowed some scope for older pupils and adults to discuss and interpret; the other tradition had an even older heritage in pre-Islamic legend, consisting of stories of Heroes, although the form in which it was mostly recalled was that of a tenth-century epic poem by Firdowsi (d. 1020) the *Shahnameh* or 'Book of Kings'. Firdowsi collected the legends of Persia relating to the country's history from before the creation of the world down to Zoroastrian times and up until the Arab conquest (636 AD). He presented them in a coherent, epic form in such simple Persian that it could still be read easily by a modern Iranian, although in the main the stories were recounted in oral form.

Although these stories were mainly known and recounted in oral tradition, they were adapted for use in school text books during the time of the Shah's modernization programmes. There was an ambivalence in this usage that reflected the dilemmas facing modernizers during this period. On the one hand the stories were used in order to reinforce a sense of a distinctive Iranian tradition, to link the modern age with the great literature of the past. On the other, it was used as an example of the 'ignorance' of the past in contrast with contemporary, scientific enlightenment. For instance, in a grade three school text book there were two accounts of the discovery of fire, one taken from *Shahnameh* and one presented in contemporary 'scientific' language. The former was treated as an imaginative, but basically simple-minded account, what the text calls 'historical legend', while the latter was represented as what we now know to be true, employing modern science in an essentialist and rather fundamentalist way. The distinction is made explicit in the questions asked of students after these passages in the exercise book. They are asked 'What is history?' and then, in clear contrast, 'What part of history is old legends?'. This might be taken, at first sight, to support Goody's contention that the acquisition of literacy provides people with a greater possibility of distinguishing between historical truth and historical fiction, since the very distinction he associates with the literacy/orality divide was set up in these books (Goody, 1968, 1977). But closer examination of the material and how it was used suggests that this conclusion would be premature.

Many city-based Iranians, for instance, would use the distinction between myth and history as a marker of their own superiority over 'primitive' villagers: they could tell 'fact' from 'legend' whereas the peasants could not. A major source of these 'facts' was the school text book: the explanation for the discovery of fire, for instance, was frequently in terms of the supposed matter-of-fact view presented there, in contrast with the poetic licence of the oral tradition and the *Shahnameh* stories. The latter, in fact, involve far greater realization of the kinds of events that may have taken place and of the human characters involved than the rather flat text book version, but these qualities are not highlighted in the new tradition which develops instead a simplistic, functionalist discourse. The text book version of the discovery of fire, for instance, deals in blurred generalizations whereby unrealized and imprecise characters such as 'primitive man' are represented in utilitarian terms as experimenting in simple-minded ways with the properties of fire and stone, the simple precursors of modern sophistication and Progress. It is within this framework of what constitutes 'facts' and 'history' that many city-dwellers see their own superiority to the backward villager, whom they perceive as lost in mists of legend and oral literature. Even were they right in their version of historical truth, such constant repetition of a sense of superiority and the use of literacy as a political weapon in urban–rural relations would, in Hoggart's terms, represent a narrowing influence. But the loss may be greater than this. The ability to empathize, to see through to the human dimension in activities that at first appear alien, is lost in generalizations about how 'primitive man' as such experimented his way towards fire, in contrast with the individually realized characterization of the oral legends that sharpens and develops such insight. It is in this sense that the consequences of literacy in Iran may bear some similarity to the debasement of sensibility described by Leavis, Hoggart and Williams in their accounts of the spread of literacy in England. As Hoggart put it, this use of written materials was more likely to train people to sympathize than to empathize, to view others in patronizing terms rather than attempting to understand them in their own terms.

All of this counters the views put forward by Jack Goody and others regarding the effects of literacy (Goody, 1968, 1977). He supposed, for instance, that the acquisition of literacy facilitated the distinction between myth and history and helped develop critical thought and scepticism. The evidence I have been considering here suggests that the contrary may have been the case: that not only does modern literacy foster uncritical belief in specific, 'modern' renderings of the world, it also contributes to a weakening of the kinds of sensibility and scepticism that may have been fostered in oral tradition. This point is reinforced if we examine the way in which the concept of kingship was represented in the literary materials disseminated under the Shah. The school text books, the magazines and official literature and the grand *jashne* or feast at Shiraz in 1975, when the Shah entertained the royal families of the world amidst a blaze of international publicity amply covered in the local newspapers, all served to represent the Iranian kingship as an unbroken line from the time of Cyrus the Great in 500 BC down to the then Shahanshah, Muhammed Reza Pahlavi. In fact the series was one of continual change, new dynasties ousting the old as conquerors from the north or just internal rivals placed themselves on the Peacock throne. This fact was well known to many Iranians before this century and probably to many under the Shah. But the newspapers in the towns and the school text books in the village presented an ideal of a continuous inheritance. History, in other words, was being re-written to suit current purposes as easily in a literate society as in oral traditions. The development of literacy in Iranian villages may have brought with it a new distinction between history and legend but the distinction did not enable them to see history any more 'objectively' than anyone else: it was itself part of an ideology. It encouraged young villagers and urban Iranians to scorn older people for 'believing' in the stories of their fathers, while they themselves believed equally strongly in the new legends.

Goody defends his claims for literacy against such counter evidence by suggesting that these are examples of 'restricted' literacy: it has not reached its full potential, as represented by western literacy, as a result of some impediment in the society. The impediment to which he pays most attention is that of religion, which thereby becomes representative of the oral side of the great divide. Nevertheless, when a religion becomes implicated in a larger network of literacy it should, according to Goody, change its character. It should for instance, lead to a generalization of formerly specific moral values –

'thou shalt not kill thy kinsman' becomes 'thou shalt not kill'. He says:

> In a literate world religion, the network of primitive classifications cannot possibly have the same correspondence with other aspects of the social structure as they have in a small-scale hunting community. In pre-literate systems different aspects of the symbolic system link up in a closer way than they do in literate societies, where they relate to a wider external range of association. (Goody, 1968, p. 5)

The contextual ambiguity associated with face-to-face discussion of specific events is, according to Goody, lost when they are written down, where the universalistic aspect is emphasized. As with the spread of a literate religion, so the spread of modern, state-centered literacy programmes have been taken as involving a similar broadening of the range of association. But, as I have argued elsewhere (Street, 1984, especially chapter 2), Goody's arguments must be approached with caution: the notion of 'broadening' associated with literacy has been overstated. In fact, the 'wider' associations of a literate religion such as Islam become part of the texture of village life, as closely enmeshed in the social structure as are religious beliefs in non-literate societies. The structure of marriage, for instance, is no less closely linked in Iranian villages to the structure of religious beliefs than it is for the Nuer and other such small-scale, 'pre-literate' communities. Modes of divorce, the rights of husband and wife, the tone of daily activity are all derived from the Qur'ān and the stories of the life of Muhammed and his followers. At weddings or on holidays in Cheshmeh there was no dancing and no playing of musical instruments, although a minority would have liked this; it was not so much that such things were banned in formal theology since in other Islamic regions the texts are interpreted in such a way as to allow them, but that they clashed with the tone and style of local realizations of Islam, which laid particular emphasis on the sadness and melancholy associated with the martyrdom of early heroes of Islam and of Imam Reza who is buried in Mashad. Pilgrimages to Mashad and re-enactments of 'passion plays' or ta'zia at certain times in memory of the murder of Hussein, the third Imam or Successor of Muhammed in the Shi'a line, are the central ritual elements of adherence to Islam in this region and they set the tone and atmosphere for daily life. The network of classifications involved in these processes clearly has close correspondence with other aspects of social structure, despite their being derived ultimately from a 'literate world religion' with its wider external range of association: local interpretations and enactments, as Hodgson points out, vary across both time and space:

> any particular formulation of thought or practice is to be seen as the result or how the everchanging setting formed by the Islamic Tradition is reflected in particular circumstances and in relation to the other cultural tradition present. (Hodgson, 1974, vol. 1, p. 85).

The acquisition of literacy on its own, then, does not necessarily effect a radical break with the previous, local forms of religious tradition, despite Goody's assertions to the contrary. Indeed, in the Iranian case the relationship between the uses of literacy and religious practice are made even more complex by the persistence of elements of an even older religious tradition, that of Zoroastrianism. Ennayat has shown how the theme of the Islamic succession story became interwoven with earlier, Zoroastrian themes of Apocalyptic revenge particularly associated with the story of Siavosh, which also appears in the *Shahnameh* (Ennayat, 1972). Recent commentators have suggested a further link between this theme and aspects of the Iranian revolution, in particular the use of martyrdom by Khumeini's regime as an ideological justification for the loss of life both in the struggle against the Shah and in the war with Iraq: the theme continues to be re-worked in both national and local terms, irrespective of its location in oral or literate channels of communication (cf. Hooglund, 1983). In the case both of the Islamic adoption of Zoroastrian themes and of the present extensions of literacy to rural areas, the external associations of a new literacy were incorporated into village life and integrated closely with existing beliefs and associations. The wider reference of an external literate world religion was localized.

The new literacy brought by State institutions and within a western ideological framework, has many of the features of a literate world religion and one might expect to see some of the same processes of adaptation and assimilation to local ideology at work. The school text book version of the Firdowsi story about the discovery of fire, for instance, did not always succeed in its attempt to put the villagers' history into a different conceptual and ontological framework than that of either Zoroastrian or Islamic belief. In these books, the accounts of the past represented in these traditions and now an integral part of local ideology were distinguished from the new account as a relationship of 'legend' to 'history', 'fiction' to 'fact'. The style of the books also contained a new ideology. Where the early stories depicted epochal events in history as mediated by distinctive individual heroes, after whom villagers might name their children and who became a part of daily consciousness, the modern story was represented in terms of impersonalized, general ancestors. Further, the present relationship with them was presented somewhat patronizingly as one of Progress beyond their simple thinking and their crude science. The new stories also involved new models of human character and morality, those of pragmatism, experimentation and technical skill rather than of the heroic qualities associated with the characters in the *Shahnameh*. To Goody the acquisition of literacy means that the villager is being asked to 'generalize' more than he was accustomed, to relate to wider external associations: the evidence under consideration here seems to suggest that the development of mass literacy through schooling does not so much represent a change at this level, from local to national, specific to general modes of thought, but rather at the level of content and ideology. The generalizations the villager is being asked to make are those of an alien, urban society; they lack that direct relation with his own social environment and beliefs that the stories of the *Shahnameh* and of the Islamic tradition have acquired over centuries of re-telling. Formerly his children would be named after the heroes of both traditions and would be encouraged to imitate their qualities of honour, pride, physical achievement, martyrdom, rigour, etc. The prime heroes of the new school text books, on the other hand, were modern utilitarians working to 'develop' a 'backward' economy and they were often enshrined in the character of the Shah himself and his family, whose photographs appeared in the introductory pages of every volume of every book. In Hoggart's terms one might interpret the uses of this new literacy as being to change honour into narrow nationalism, pride into superiority and study relevant to local belief into exam-oriented, mindless learning of alien texts for promotion into a different world. Whereas Goody sees literacy as having the potential to develop objective thought and such distinctions as that between history and legend, an analysis in the style of the 'culture and society' tradition would balance the picture by demonstrating the limiting effects some literacies may have. The change from rote learning of the Qur'ān and recounting stories of the *Shahnameh* to rote learning of school text books and their stories of man's material progress, may represent a less significant achievement than is often claimed for the new literacy.

However, the villager is no more simply indoctrinated by such government texts than the working class in England by the mass literature and magazines that Hoggart and Williams describe. As with the assimilation of Islam in Zoroastrian times, so under the Shah the beliefs and myths associated with modern literacy were incorporated and adapted into local perceptions. For instance, the scientific achievements of the West, about which students learned through school text books, the radio and cinema and often represented by pinning photographs of such events as the moon landing on mud walls, were assimilated by villagers into their religious framework. All of the achievements from the moon landing to television were, they maintained, predicted in the Qur'ān and could be found in the text by careful examination. The West may have stolen a lead in technological development but immediate gains were to be seen in the perspective of Islamic world history. It was this kind of thinking that provided much of the ideological underpinnings for the revolution towards the end of the 1970s and which was missed during the early 1970s by western-oriented modernizers intent on their own vision of the new Iran. It was assumed, for instance, by many villagers and by students who had acquired some western education but wanted to incorporate it into their Islamic belief rather than use it to undermine that belief, that once the technical skills had been acquired Muslims would forge ahead of the West because of the moral strength of Islam. I was frequently asked in the village why the West remained so far behind in its religious development when it had achieved so much in other fields. In the history of Islam prophets succeeded one another, each one rendering the previous one's teaching obsolete. Earlier prophets like Abraham and Christ were respected and their teachings revered up to a point, but they were all superseded by Muhammed who gave the direct word of God to man in the Holy Qur'ān. In this sense Christians were 'old-fashioned', as much behind the times in an Iranian villager's eyes as they themselves were deemed to be by English villagers or some urban Iranians. The new knowledge was being assimilated to existing patterns, just as Islam itself had been incorporated into some of the traditional patterns of Iranian life and of Zoroastrian belief centuries before. The new literacy, to the extent that it was part of a process of social change, altered the content rather than the mode of perception.

There are many other ways in which the changes associated with the new literacy could be shown as less dramatic and radical than Goody and others have assumed, but I am simply concerned here to provide some suggestions as to how the process might be interpreted rather than to provide a comprehensive survey. I have tried to suggest ways in which an anthropologist, working in the cultural studies tradition and others who have made use of literary critical styles of analysis, might consider the effects of new literacies. I have tried to document in relation to particular villages in Iran during the early 1970s the kinds of processes that Lienhardt and Al-Shahi have described for education in general in contemporary Middle Eastern society (Lienhardt, 1980; Al-Shahi, 1980). In relation to some of the theoretical debates about literacy and social change, I have suggested that the significance attributed to literacy by Goody and others might be balanced by the limitations pointed out by writers like Hoggart. For every example that Goody brings forward of literacy effecting profound changes in perception or social structure, we can document cases where the opposite is the case – where the ideas expressed in the literature made newly available were incorporated into existing frameworks of thought and where the uses made of literacy were assimilated to the existing social structure. The emphasis should be, then, not on literacy *per se* but on content and ideology.

If this is the case and if anthropologists are beginning to go to the field prepared to analyze the content of the texts their subjects are reading, whether school books, newspapers, comics, magazines, notices or whatever, then they might gain something from an acquaintance with the similar work conducted in England, within the literary critical tradition, regarding the uses of literacy. This would require some knowledge of the central literary tradition in the country studied, including the background of those who produce the literature read in villages by the newly literate. In addition it involves attention to strands of earlier traditions that have long been incorporated into oral tradition in the countryside and are now being re-inserted there via texts written from a different ideological perspective. In Iran literacy was taught in the context of national policies, themselves the product of specific ideological and literary traditions. The relation of such general aspects of the wider society that brings literacy to the village, to local beliefs and patterns of thought and behaviour, need to be analyzed. I have suggested one or two ways in which this might be done through a brief consideration of some of the school text books being used in Iranian villages during the 1970s and their relationship to both local and national traditions. Such an approach owes something to my own background in English Literature before moving to anthropology where, as Peter Lienhardt and a number of others who have come a similar route have pointed out, there is scope for a fruitful combination of literary critical and anthropological approaches and ideas.

References

Al-Shahi, Ahmed (1980) 'Educational Cross-Currents,' *Bulletin of British Society for Middle East Studies*, vol. 7, no. 2.

Arasteh, R. (1964) *Education and Social Awakening in Iran*. Brill: Leiden.

Bharier, J. (1971) *Economic Development in Iran, 1900–1970*. OUP: Oxford.

Centre for Contemporary Cultural Studies (1978) *On Ideology*. Hutchinson: London.

Ennayat, H. (1972) Public Lecture at Middle East Centre, Oxford.

Goody, J. (ed.) (1968) *Literacy in Traditional Societies*. CUP: Cambridge.

Goody, J. (1977) *The Domestication of the Savage Mind*. CUP: Cambridge.

Hashemi, M.G. (1966) 'Adult Education in Rural Iran: problems and prospects', MA thesis, Department of Education of the American University of Beirut, Lebanon.

Hodgson, M. (1974) *The Venture of Islam*, 3 vols. Chicago UP: Chicago, Illinois.

Hoggart, R. (1957) *The Uses of Literacy*. Penguin: London.

Hooglund, M. (1983) 'Two Images of Husain: Accommodation and Revolution in an Iranian Village', in N. Keddie (ed.) *Religion and Politics in Iran*. Yale UP: New Haven, Connecticut.

Lienhardt, P.A. (1980) 'Facts, Theories and Values in Middle Eastern Education', *Bulletin of British Society for Middle East Studies*, vol. 7, no. 2.

Ministry of Education, Iran, Text Books for Dabestan (Primary School).

Pahlavi, H.I.M. Mohammamed Reza Shah (1960) *Mission for My Country*. Hutchinson: London.

Seddigh Gharib, G. (1966) 'Training Teachers for Rural Elementary Schools in Iran', MA thesis, American University of Beirut, Lebanon.

Street, B. (1975) 'The *Mullāh*, the *Shahnameh* and the *Madrasseh*: Some Aspects of Literacy in Iran', *Asian Affairs*, vol. 62.

Street, B. (1984) *Literacy in Theory and Practice*. CUP: Cambridge.

Street, B. (1987) 'Literacy and Social Change: The Significance of Social Context in the Development of Literary Programmes', in D. Wagner (ed.) *The Future of Literacy in a Changing World*. Pergamon Press: Oxford.

Street, B. (1993) ' "Culture is a Verb": Anthropological Aspects of Language and Cultural Process', in D. Graddol, L. Thompson and M. Byram (eds) *Language and Culture*. Multilingual Matters/BAAL: Clevedon, Philadelphia.

Williams, R. (1958) *Culture and Society*. Penguin: London.

Williams, R. (1961) *The Long Revolution*. Chatto: London.

4 Orality and Literacy as Ideological Constructions: Some Problems in Cross-Cultural Studies

I have argued in the opening section of this book that much of the earlier study of literacy was grounded in narrow conceptions of what literacy meant in western culture. As we have seen, in both the academic and the applied, development literature, the underlying assumptions about the nature of literacy were often derived from the particular literacy practices of the observer's own culture, and their own academic subculture within it, with its emphasis, for instance, on 'essay-text' uses of literacy and on 'literary' prose. These assumptions were associated with a more general faith in the rationality, 'objectivity' and logic imbued by western education systems, and in particular by their unique literacy practices, which for many were the source of 'Progress' and Scientific Achievement in western society since the Enlightenment. By implication, 'other cultures', lacking western literacy and the education and progress that went with it, lacked 'enlightenment' (see Bloch, 1989). Similarly, earlier periods of western history were 'dark ages' in which the light of reason was only kept burning by a few *literate* 'clerics' (see Clanchy, 1979).

Within a framework such as this, the study of the transition from orality to literacy in 'other cultures' tended to be a study of how far 'they' were becoming like 'us': since 'we', with our forms of literacy, have achieved such technological marvels as putting men on the moon, the acquisition of such literacy by others means that it is only a matter of time until they 'catch up'. It is in this fundamentally ethnocentric sense that literacy has tended to be viewed almost entirely in positive terms. As Hamilton and Barton point out: 'Literacy is equated with progress and via literacy benefits accrue to nations and individuals. As a result, levels of literacy in a society are hypothesised to correlate positively with any and all indicators of social and economic progress. As Graff says "the uses of literacy are still debated: its basic value is not"' (quoted in Hamilton and Barton, 1985).

Hamilton and Barton's wide-ranging survey of approaches to literacy in recent years is able to cite a number of writers who have rejected this ethnocentric view of literacy and, indeed, Graff's own work has gone a long way towards establishing a climate in which the 'basic value' of literacy *can* be debated. The study of literacy in cross-cultural perspective (across both time and space) requires some such broad framework, free of the assumption that what literacy on its own will necessarily achieve is the same in all times and places and that, with all 'restrictions off' it will always manifest itself, in the same way as it has done in western cultures. This book, citing work conducted within this broader framework (see especially: Wagner, 1987; Schieffelin and Gilmore, 1986; Reder and Green, 1983; Heath, 1983; Finnegan, 1988; Shuman, 1986; Street, 1984) and adopting an ethnographic approach to the study of literacy, demonstrates the sheer variety and complexity of literate and oral practices.

Such cross-cultural study is, however, notoriously complex and uncertain and before developing the argument for it any further it is important to record and analyze some of the problems that anthropologists have encountered in attempting to apply their discipline to the investigation of literacy in different times and places. I do so, not in order to criticize individuals, many of whom have made important contributions to such enquiry, but rather to suggest ways in which certain common misconceptions and methodological confusions may be avoided in future.

I begin with a consideration of a classic procedure of nineteenth-century anthropology known as the 'if I were a horse' approach to other cultures, which I suggest remains implicit in many contemporary studies of literacy and which has helped to reinforce the emphasis on peculiarly western forms of literacy at the expense of the variety of indigenous practices across the world. Lienhardt explains the meaning of this approach in his account of its use by the 'armchair' anthropologist Sir James Frazer at the turn of the century:

Frazer's psychological insight, on which he prided himself, was often at fault, largely because he thought that he could understand very foreign beliefs quite out of their real contexts simply by an effort of introspection. He and others of his time had something of the approach of Sherlock Holmes in the work of his near-contemporary Conan Doyle: 'You know my methods in such cases, Watson: I put myself in the man's place, and having first gauged his intelligence, I try to imagine how I myself should have proceeded under the same circumstances'. (Lienhardt, 1964, p. 27)

In fact all analysis of other modes of thought and belief involves some such procedures, in the sense that it attempts to represent the underlying coherence and 'rationality' of apparently strange assertion and behaviour, and the researcher attempts to put him or herself into the thinking of their subject. But such an approach requires close knowledge of that subject's social context and of the institutions which give meaning to their ideas and beliefs, if it is to avoid crude ethnocentrism. As Lienhardt says: 'Such deductive procedures might have their merits in the study of people with whom the investigator had much in common. They could only mislead where the student was a middle-class Victorian scholar and the subject an Australian aborigine or an ancient Egyptian priest' (Lienhardt, 1964, p. 27). One might add, or a person employing non-western forms of literacy.

I would like to suggest that the 'if I were a horse' approach lies at the heart of much of the academic work on literacy. Exponents of the 'autonomous' model of literacy, as we have seen, have attempted to treat literacy as an independent variable, supposedly detached from its social context, and then to 'read off' its consequences in terms which correspond remarkably closely to the 'if I were a horse' thinking of the nineteenth-century anthropologists. The major 'consequence' of literacy has, then, been that it 'facilitates' logic, rationality, objectivity and rational thinking (cf. Goody, 1968, 1977; Ong, 1977, 1982a and b; Olson, 1977), arguments that I have criticized above, especially in Section 1. By implication, those without literacy would appear therefore to lack these qualities and, indeed, in popular usage 'illiterate' is often taken to mean just this, namely 'illogical', 'irrational' etc. In colonial times those non-European societies that lacked western forms of literacy were seen as thereby lacking rationality, logic etc., both as social wholes and in terms of the individuals that made up such societies. Their rituals and beliefs were seen as evidence that they were 'unscientific' and incapable of detached reflection on their state of being. Sir James Frazer (1890), for instance, employing 'if I were a horse' procedures in his collations of evidence from cultures around the world, had imagined that other peoples were at an earlier stage of mental evolution, that they believed literally in their magical rites and that they could be characterized as 'pre-logical' in their thinking. Elements of these assumptions have continued in twentieth-century encounters with non-European societies and I would like to look in particular at some of these in terms of the light they throw on the perception and study of literacy. In particular I shall be examining some of the more dramatic examples of indigenous response to European invasion that are represented in the literature under the general heading of 'cargo cults', and which, through the role played in them by literacy beliefs and practices, provide a useful test case for the analysis of literacy across cultures.

'Cargo cults' are documented particularly in Melanesia during the early part of this century and occurred where local responses to European control of goods and resources took the form of cult movements attempting to commandeer this 'cargo' for the indigenous population. Such movements included, on occasions, the adoption of certain forms of the literacy introduced by Europeans, often through missionary schools, in ways which would emphasize local interests and beliefs rather than those of the colonists. The accounts of these indigenous uses of literacy are often couched, I would argue, in terms of the 'autonomous' model of literacy and are based upon 'if I were a horse' approaches. They represent, then, particularly dramatic examples of the assumptions that underlie, often implicitly, a great many accounts of the transition from orality to literacy in the contemporary world.

One of the most detailed accounts of the role of literacy in cargo cults is provided by the social anthropologist John Clammer in his *Literacy and Social Change: a Case Study of Fiji* (1976). Literacy was first brought to Fiji in 1835 by two Wesleyan missionaries, William Cross and David Cargill. These men had spent some time previously on Tonga, another Polynesian island, where they had learnt the local language and developed an appreciation of the importance for successful conversion of learning native languages, compiling dictionaries and producing written material. By the time they arrived they had already translated a portion of the catechism into Fijian and had their Tongan press print the text. In 1838 a printing press was set up in Fiji itself, as more proselytes of the Wesleyan Methodist Missionary Society arrived. The Wesleyans saw evangelizing as indissolubly linked with the provision of education and 'functional' literacy. 'Functional' literacy in this context meant the ability to read and

understand basic Christian Scriptures, as translated into the vernacular. It is reported that the Fijians showed considerable reluctance to
abandon traditional religious practices but that they flocked to the
support of the first educational projects. In nine months the missionaries at Lakemba got 122 pupils but no converts. Since, however, the
only reading material being made available was Christian texts, the
foundation was being laid for later successful conversion. The only
texts available in the Bau dialect, for instance, were twelve pages of
the no. 2 conference catechism (Clammer, 1976, p.54) and the alphabet in print.

Learning to read thus involved Fijians in becoming acquainted
with Christian thought and coming under mission tutelage. That
tutelage involved uses of literacy learning for disciplinary and social
control purposes. Testing was common and emphasized the reading
of Scriptures and the chanting of questions and answers. On one
occasion a visitor described the way in which traditional ritual
swaying and chanting had been adapted to school learning so that a
geography lesson was 'a series of chanted questions and answers
which, however musical, can scarcely be expected to convey much
meaning to the mind of the Fijian' (Clammer, 1976, p. 65). Manghubai
points out that 'if the geography lesson were indeed a series of
chants, then what the Fijians were doing was simply taking something
that was foreign to their culture and adapting it to their patterns
where chants were often a conveyance of history from one generation
to another' (Manghubai, 1985a). The visitor, and Clammer in his
account of these events, pay little attention to such possibilities,
instead concentrating on an implicit notion of 'meaning' as cotermin-
ous with western conceptions of rationality and logic. The teachers,
moreover, were not interested in either the local adaptations of
European pedagogy or in conveying such general 'meaning' as the
visitor seems to have had in mind. The Wesleyan missionaries were
concerned rather with gaining converts and maintaining their position. As Clammer points out they held 'a very low opinion of native
mentality' which manifested itself in 'the setting of an almost equally
low educational level'. He tells us that the missionaries

> . . . did nothing to encourage the growth of indigenous institutions and
> only educated the native to the extent of making the intelligent
> dissatisfied at their inability to progress beyond basic skills, no provi-
> sion being made for anything further . . . (Clammer, 1976, p. 61)

What the Fijians were getting as their experience of literacy, then, was an insensitive and authoritarian teaching in the most superficial levels of European Christian thought. There is nothing in that experience to suggest that literacy will, of its nature, lift those who learn it out of their 'socially embedded' contexts as Goody and others seem to expect (Goody, 1977; Olson, 1977; Ong, 1982a). It can, in fact, be used to do just the opposite, to embed pupils deeply in the ideology and social control of the teacher's social class and deliberately prevent them from arriving at a detached and critical appraisal of their real situation. Goody in fact takes account of such exceptions to his 'claims' for the intellectual and critical advantages of literacy by designating them 'restricted' literacy, but that of course is merely circular (Goody, 1968; see above, chapter 3).

The ideological basis for the uses of texts for wider political control can be seen from an examination of the colonists' own descriptions of the process of imparting literacy to the Fijians and of the natives' response to it. Henderson, for instance, in *Fiji and the Fijians* (1931) writes that the natives came to the mission schools because they wanted, among other things, 'the printing press that made those wonderful books that had strange marks in them by which people could talk to others far away' (p. 56). The language here supposedly represents the quality of thought; it is awe-struck – 'wonderful', 'strange' and simple-minded – 'talk to others far away'. A representation of Henderson's own uses of literacy for communication over time and space would not be likely to use such patronizing expressions. The idea that letters appear like 'strange marks' to the natives underestimates the familiarity that those in the classes must have soon acquired with the alphabet and with written forms. What they passed on to others not yet attending the classes was likely to be more pragmatic accounts of the way in which written letters could be used to represent words and some of the excitement that accompanies the recognition of the intellectual and political implications of the transmission of messages over time and space. Clammer, however, in citing Henderson fails to put his comments into such perspective but instead lends authority to their patronizing tone by reproducing it in his own language. He describes, for instance, the Fijians' interest in learning literacy as a desire to be admitted to the 'secrets of the Europeans' mysterious symbolic script'.

There is, in fact, no need to appeal to such terms nor to attempt to 'get inside' the native mind in the narrow version of the 'if I were a horse' tradition employed by both Clammer and Henderson, in order to understand the importance of literacy to indigenous peoples in the nineteenth century. Even in the distorted missionary texts that we have available we can find sufficient evidence of real social practices in relation to literacy to uncover the ideological and political significance of literacy for the local population.

One example of such material is a passage regarding the relationship of Wesleyan missionaries to the people of Raratonga in the Cook Islands, quoted by Clammer from *A Narrative of Missionary Enterprises* written by J. Williams in 1837. Clammer's introduction to the passage again reinforces the representation of native awe and mystery provided by the missionaries themselves. Clammer writes:

> The mystique of books and the wonder at the power of writing is recorded by Williamson on Raratonga, which was included within the Wesleyans' religious auspices. (Clammer, 1980, p. 66)

The passage reads:

> In the erection of this chapel, a circumstance occurred which will give a striking idea of the feelings of an untaught people, when observing for the first time, the effects of written communication. As I had come to the work one morning without my square, I took up a chip, and with a piece of charcoal wrote upon it a request that Mrs Williams should send me that article. I called a chief who was superintending his portion of the work, and said to him 'Friend take this; go to our house and give it to Mrs Williams'. He was a singular looking man, remarkably quick in his movements and had been a great warrior: but in one of the numerous battles he had fought, had lost an eye. Giving me an inexpressible look with the other, he said 'Take that – she will call me a fool and scold me, if I carry a chip to her'. 'No' I replied 'she will not; take it and go immediately; I am in haste'. Perceiving me to be in earnest, he took it and asked 'What must I say?' I replied 'You have nothing to say; the chip will say all I wish'. With a look of astonishment and contempt, he held up the piece of wood and said 'How can this speak? has this a mouth?'. I desired him to take it immediately, and not spend so much time in talking about it. On arriving at the house, he gave the chip to Mrs Williams, who read it, threw it away, and went to the tool chest; whither the chief, resolving to see the result of this mysterious proceeding, followed her closely. On receiving the square from her, he said, 'Stay daughter, how do you

know that this is what Mr Williams wants?' 'Why' she replied, 'did you not bring me a chip just now?' 'Yes', said the astonished warrior, 'but I did not hear it say anything'. 'If you did not, I did', was the reply, 'for it made known to me what he wanted, and all you have to do is return with it as quickly as possible'. With this the chief leaped out of the house; and catching up the mysterious piece of wood, he ran through the settlement with the chip in one hand and the square in the other, holding them up as high as his arms would reach, and shouting as he went, 'See the Wisdom of these English people; they can make chips talk! they can make chips talk!' On giving me the square, he wished to know how it was possible thus to converse with persons at a distance. I gave him all the explanation in my power; but it was a circumstance involved in so much mystery, that he actually tied a string to the chip, hung it round his neck, and wore it for some time. During several following days, we frequently saw him surrounded by a crowd, who were listening with some interest while he narrated the wonders which this chip had performed. (Clammer, 1976, p. 67)

Shorn of its colonial overtones, this passage could be taken as evidence of the sense of intellectual discovery and excitement that the acquisition of literacy can provide and a demonstration that local peoples were quick to understand the potential of literacy despite the narrow ways in which it was being made known to them. We can, then, make sense of this passage without having to appeal to mystification of literacy itself and to the assumptions about native irrationality, typical of a nineteenth-century text.

The missionary here had already provided the chief with a metaphor with which to represent the meaning of literacy by remarking 'the chip will *say* all I wish' (my emphasis). He should hardly have been surprised, then, when the chief shouted 'they can make chips talk'. Yet clearly the chief's response and action are represented as foolish and child-like. Similarly, there is no necessary mystery about the process of learning how to write on a chip, but the account here suggests that it is 'a circumstance, involved in much mystery'. Rather than relating it to the mundane learning practices of the missionary schools, where it was being daily acquired by the chief's countrymen, Williams seems to have 'explained' it to the chief in a way that further mystified it. The tone of the passage would suggest that this mystification was part of a general attempt by such writers to establish and maintain a position of superiority over the natives. The chief is treated as a servant; his interest in the process in which he is told to help is represented in patronizing terms as though one could not expect natives to understand much; his excited response to the real discovery of the power of writing is scorned – 'he *actually* tied a string to the chip' (my emphasis).

That tone gives us an indication of what indigenous populations had to endure from the Europeans. It also provides a sense of what the context was like in which they first encountered literacy. What literacy is for any group is what it is in the contexts in which they experience it. In this context they could not help but experience literacy as embedded in the social institutions of hierarchy and political power. The missionary in his 'explanation' of literacy to the chief made that clear. Also, his use of the written word to pass an order to his wife and her compliance with it provided an indication for the chief of the potential significance of literacy for the excercise of power. If the missionary could use it in this way with regard to a person subject to his commands, then so too could chiefs with regard to their subjects. Further, the bureaucracies which Europeans constructed to establish their rule were clearly based on these same aspects of writing, the communication of messages and orders over time and space, within a hierarchical framework. Recognition of these aspects is manifest in the 'cargo cults' which developed in Melanesia in the twentieth century and which made considerable use of literacy practices in their challenge to European hegemony. The scene described by Williams could be taken as a precursor of these more fully developed political uses of literacy (which I describe in greater detail below). The crowds gathered round the chief represented, in fact, a threat to continued European control. Williams' scorn was short-sighted.

This scene, then, need not be interpreted as evidence of native awe at the 'mystery' of literacy, as Williams and Clammer suggest. It can be seen, instead, as the foundation of specific ideological and political perceptions of literacy by a colonized population, many of which have revolutionary potential. As a result of such scenes and such perceptions, many local people flocked to the missionaries' classes. They went in order to obtain from the Europeans one of the key sources of their wealth and power.

However, having arrived in the schools, they found themselves being provided with only a mystified version of literacy practice, that served to maintain their subordination rather than opening new doors to the wealth they saw displayed by Europeans. They consequently continued to recognize that something was being withheld from them. That difference in interpretation between the two groups was the soil in which indigenous experience of literacy grew. The awe and confusion, in which indigenous peoples are represented as being, stemmed from the tantalizing way in which they were being offered literate practices rather than from any intellectual shortcomings or 'mystical' thought on their part. By emphasizing that awe and confusion rather than either analyzing its social causes or even criticizing the representation of native thought that generates over-attention to such concepts, Clammer tends to understate the ideological aspect of local conceptions of literacy.

This is also apparent if we examine his account of how the actual practice of *writing* was acquired. Again he quotes Williams and accepts the patronizing tone uncritically:

> We taught them first to write by means of sand-boards, but, of course, they could not by this mode acquire any great facility in the art. They frequently expressed their regret at this and, as our supply of slates was very small, they determined if possible, to find substitutes. Having formed the resolution they were observed once more, on leaving the school, running in groups up the mountains and shortly returning with flakes of stones, which they had broken off from rocks. These they carried to the seabeach and rubbed with sand and coral until they had produced a smooth surface. Thus far successful, they coloured the stones with the purple juice of the mountain plantain, to give them the appearance of English slates. Some of the boys completed the resemblance by cutting them square and framing them so that without close examination you could scarely detect the difference. The next desideratum was a pencil and for this they went into the sea and procured a number of the echinus or sea-urchin, which is armed with twenty or thirty spines. These they burnt slightly to render them soft, that they might not scratch; and with these flakes of stone for a slate and the spine of a sea-urchin for a pencil, they wrote exceedingly well; and hundreds of them took down the principal portions of every discourse they heard. (Quoted in Clammer, 1976, p. 68)

This could be interpreted as a significant and dramatic account of a people's attempt to command the material means of communication from within an institutional framework geared simply to their role as passive consumers of text rather than active producers of their own literate practice. Their activities would then compare interestingly with the attempts by some involved in contemporary English Adult

Literacy provision for instance, to create the conditions in which those acquiring literacy produce their own texts. This involves students in first creating their own literary material and then themselves producing it as text in material form through the processes of writing, editing, printing, binding, and book production and distribution.

In nineteenth-century Melanesia, however, those responsible for literacy provision worked within a different ideology. They were concerned to limit both the content and the practice of literacy. Since the missionaries saw literacy practice as a means simply to conversion and to social control, they had no interest in providing any more than was necessary for this bare minimum. Teaching reading rather than writing was generally sufficient for this purpose, so that what writing was taught was severely limited in terms both of the materials the mission were prepared to make available and the uses to which they were prepared to see them put. As Williams states, students 'could not by this mode acquire any great facility in the art'. However, the passage suggests that some students were attempting to break free of these constraints. Writing can involve a greater degree of authorial control over what is written than the reader tends to have over what is read. Where, in addition, writers have their own materials they are less easily directed than the reader for whom control of texts by the supplier can be total. The people in the account appear to have been learning something of this. One might infer that in taking down with their own materials, 'the principal portions of every discourse they heard', they were recording non-religious as well as religious affairs and becoming practised in indigenous control of their own literacy, both in form and content.

Williams' patronizing representation of the way in which his students created their own material means of communication misses this aspect of their activities. Similarly, Clammer cites the passage simply to indicate native 'zeal' for literacy and fails to counteract the colonial overtones or to develop the positive implications. As in his treatment of the earlier passage by Williams, Clammer's representation of what literacy meant to the local people is constrained by his implicit acceptance of significant features of the autonomous model of literacy. That model entails representing the meaning of literacy practices for Melanesian peoples in terms of limited mental operations. These are deduced by the European observer from assumptions about how he himself would respond to such new and strange phenomena if he were a member of a 'primitive' society. This approach to the modes of thought of other societies derives in part, as we have seen, from the 'if I were a horse' tradition. The 'autonomous' model, of its nature, emphasizes what Lienhardt describes as the more 'misleading' and ethnocentric aspects of this method. In the Melanesian case this leads to representation of the natives as over-awed by 'the Europeans' mysterious symbolic script' and by 'the mystique of books and wonder at the power of writing'. The flaw in this version of the tradition, and in the representation of local perceptions of literacy that stems from it, lies in the lack of attention to the social structures within which the concepts and philosophies of specific cultures are formed and in the deductive, ethnocentric nature of the assumptions made about the thinking processes of other peoples. It might be feasible to say, 'If I were a Melanesian then literacy would have these particular meanings', if we knew more of these specific structures and beliefs, as Lienhardt points out.

Clammer, indeed, is aware of the conditions in which 'if I were a horse' interpretation is appropriate and he does elsewhere attempt to describe the social structure of Fiji in such a way as to make sense of local Fijian responses to European rule. But where he employs secondary accounts of Melanesian responses to the literacy practices brought by the Europeans, as in Williams' account of Raratonga and Henderson's of Fiji, he seems to abandon that awareness and to reproduce the language and concepts of the 'if I were a horse' tradition, and of the ethnocentric features of it that Lienhardt exposes. I would argue that he does so because he implicitly employs the 'autonomous' model of literacy which is itself grounded in those features. By not making explicit the model of literacy that he is using Clammer fails to give sufficient attention to the underlying theoretical influences that are shaping his representation of Melanesian life and thought and is laying himself open therefore to the adverse consequences of the autonomous model that we noted above.

If the recognition of the ideological and political significance of local literacy practices has to be extracted in the way I have attempted, from these early descriptions of Melanesian responses to missionary literacy, it should have been more apparent to observers of later responses, such as the 'cargo cults', which were more explicitly political. However, we find that although their political dimension is recognized to some extent, accounts of the uses of literacy in the cults continue to emphasize the supposed cognitive deficiencies of the native mind and thereby serve to understate their ideological and political significance.

Clammer explains the growth of cargo cults in Fiji, for instance, as stemming from disillusion with the broken promises of the Europeans and a strong understanding of their relative deprivation by the natives themselves. The Fijians felt a deep-seated sense of grievance at the contrast between the Europeans' control of the cargo brought in European ships and the wealth and power that went with it, and their own penury and subservience. When the missionaries first came it had seemed that their offer of Christian education was an offer of the key to their material well-being – to 'cargo'. Fijians had been persuaded to acquire literacy which ultimately led to the abandonment of traditional religion and conversion to Christianity. They then found themselves deprived both of wealth and of traditional belief and securities. The frustration that this created began to focus in more institutionalized ways at the turn of the century, with the emergence of 'cargo cults', many of which took the form of quasi-Christian rituals, mimicking of European practices and occasionally re-enactment of some of the literacy practices employed by the colonists.

Clammer stresses the importance of these literate practices in such cults, an aspect not given much attention in other descriptions of them. One such cult was called 'Luve-ni-wai' or 'Children of the Water' after the spirits alleged to inhabit the forests and pools, possession by which was a prerequisite for joining the movement. This movement was less millenarian and, according to Clammer, less anti-white than many, being 'more of a youth movement than a take-over bid for white supremacy' (Clammer, 1976, p. 113). Colonial administrators attempted to make it 'official' by emphasizing its sports organization and youth participation. However, this forced the more radical sections of the movement underground where they adopted an organizational structure based partly on European ranks and literacy. The new 'clubs' that developed in this way adopted a hierarchy which included such functionaries as Governors, Chief Justices, Home Secretaries and Elders. These clubs laid great stress on books, records, codes of signals and other written paraphernalia. 'The material correlates of literacy, such as books, were incorporated into the "Luve-ni-wai" cult even though the movement had no written sources of its own.' Clammer says of the cults:

Their elaborate hierarchical leadership with its ranks borrowed from the government and military, was bolstered by a veritable bureaucracy of scribes with books, registers, codes and written documents of all kinds. Secretaries, treasurers and other keepers of records appeared in the ruling elite of the *Luve-ni-wai* clubs. (p. 126)

Similarly, the Tuka cult laid great emphasis on writing both in the sayings of its prophet, Ndugomi, and in its organizational framework, with 'scribes' among the hierarchy of officials and Bible references prominent. These practices are described by Clammer as 'ritualized literacy'. This concept is central to his general analysis of native religion and it is here that it becomes apparent how significant the model of literacy being used is for the analysis of other aspects of indigenous practice being described. What Clammer means by 'ritualized literacy' has to be understood in terms of the contrast he draws with 'secular literacy'. That 'secular literacy', it turns out, has many of the characteristics that were claimed, more explicitly, for literacy within the 'autonomous' model of literacy.

Clammer describes how the 'ritualized' uses of literacy developed in Fiji by reference to traditional religious practice. The native religion was pragmatic and materialistic, he writes, and only communicated with the supernatural in ritualized, oracular transactions aimed at getting material benefits. Christianity, in contrast, claimed to be able to communicate directly with the deity through spiritual means that led to some state of grace. The hidden premise, certainly as interpreted by the Fijians, was that the adoption of Christianity would also lead to material equality with the rich and powerful Christians, as represented by the missionaries. The missionaries emphasized as part of the process of conversion 'the penetration of the mysteries of the written word, providing opportunities to interpret Scriptures and to participate in the activities of the economically powerful traders not to mention the miraculous ability to convey information over time and space'. This 'exaggerated respect for the written word' was usually, claims Clammer, manifested in formalized and ritual fashion. He quotes Meggitt writing on Melanesian cargo cults in support of this hypothesis:

Thus from the beginning of their contacts with missions, many Melanesians displayed a curiously ritualized (yet practically understandable) attitude towards literacy. They took writing to be merely one more of

those inherently ambiguous modes of communication with the supernatural with which they were already familiar. From this point of
view, the virtue of writing lay in men's ability to manipulate it as an
entity in a defined ritual fashion so that they could get a grip on the
mission god and force from him his secrets. Indeed, writing soon came
to be, in itself, an important symbol of the very goals of wealth and
authority to which people aspired. Many regarded words as simply
aspects of the Word, a mark of impending millenium (sic) and a 'Road
to Cargo'. (Cargo here meant not merely commodities but the combina-
tions of wealth and power visible in the new socio-economic order.)
At any rate, it seems that writing was rarely treated as a straightforward technique of secular action, one of whose prime values is
repeated and surrogate communication of unambiguous meanings in a
variety of situations. (Meggitt, 1968, p. 32)

Meggitt, then, contrasts a 'ritualized' attitude towards literacy, mistak-
enly held by natives, with a model of literacy, implicitly assumed to
be the correct one, that he describes as 'secular' and which is clearly
very similar to the 'autonomous' model as outlined above.

The 'autonomous' model of literacy, as we have seen, assumes
that writing facilitates the 'logical' functions of language, enables
them to be separated from interpersonal functions so that written
utterances are less socially 'embedded', and therefore creates a more
objective and scientific use of language. Meggitt tests Melanesian
perceptions of literacy against just such assumptions. His claim that
the natives took writing to be 'merely' inherently ambiguous assumes
that they missed its 'true' nature, which Meggitt, echoing Goody and
others, takes to be lack of ambiguity, 'repeated and surrogate communication of unambigous meanings'. The idea that writing could be
manipulated in ritual fashion is, likewise, represented as proof of
lack of real understanding of its nature which, according to the
autonomous model, must be its ability to detach meaning *per se* from
such social manipulation. That Meggitt culls these notions of what
literacy should be and what its nature is from a shared ideology is
apparent from the fact that he feels no need to make the argument
any more explicit or more fully worked out. He simply assumes that
his readers agree in the representation of writing as a 'straightforward
technique of secular action' and that it is against such a model of
literacy that native perceptions must be held up and, inevitably,
found wanting. As we noted above, such descriptions of literacy are
not, in fact, as 'straightforward' and 'neutral' as they are claimed to

be and one might have expected the anthropologists to recognize such notions as themselves problematic.

Clammer, however, cites such assertions by Meggitt with approval and, far from problematizing them, uses them to emphasize his own comments upon 'ritualized' uses of literacy in Fijian cargo cults. He finds it odd, for instance, that the 'desacralized nature of the written word never seems to have occurred to the cult members'. If by 'desacralized' he means desocialized, unembedded in the sense used by Goody and others in their claims that writing disengages utterances from their social contexts, then one might retort that, on the contrary, it is strange that the socially embedded nature of the written word seems not to have occurred to Clammer and the other social anthropologists. That Clammer does conceive of 'desacralized' or 'true' literacy in similar terms to those used by Goody in describing the qualities of writing is made clear by his comments on another anthropologist's analysis of cargo cults. In this case he cites Kenelm Burridge's description of the uses of literacy in cargo cults among the Tangu:

> Tangu associate a 'pas' (i.e. a letter) with action, with trouble, with the triggering of a fresh series of events. Though all know what is written on a 'pas' is normally merely a substitute for an oral communication there is also a feeling that a 'pas' has efficacy sui generis, which words do not have . . . Whatever kind of origin cargo might have, the 'pas' is part of a cluster of techniques required to obtain it. (Clammer, 1976, p. 128)

Clammer comments that the use of literacy described here indicates a 'failure' to perceive anomaly'. Tangu confuse the 'mere' substitution for oral communication, that Clammer takes to be the obvious feature of writing, with social and interpersonal functions of the concrete means of communication. It is in this sense that he understands Melanesian uses of literacy to be 'ritualized'; that is in contrast with a concept of literacy as capable of perceiving anomaly, as 'context free' and 'logical' in Clammer's terms 'desacralized'. It would appear, then, that the anthropologists' reference to 'secular', 'straightforward', 'technical' uses of literacy are appeals to an implicit model that corresponds closely to that made explicit by Goody and others.

If we were to apply, instead, what I have labelled the 'ideological' model of literacy, then a different picture of native religion, of native participation in cargo cults and of native uses of literacy would emerge. I shall employ this model to deal with just three aspects of these writers' conceptualizations of literacy – the significance of form as opposed to content, the notion of manipulation of literacy forms, and the emphasis on lack of ambiguity as a feature of 'true' literacy.

Form and Content

In relation to Burridge's material, for instance, the recognition of the significance of form as well as content could be used to suggest a different reading than that offered by Clammer. Tangu uses of 'pas' or letters could be taken as a recognition, whether implicit or explicit, of the political and status implications of the form of the written word. Writing down what is said in some such conventional form as a letter, does, in fact, alter its significance; the letter is not 'merely a substitute for oral communication', a notion promulgated by early linguists such as Bloomfield (1933) but since rejected by his successors (cf. Stubbs, 1980). The material form is not as 'transparent' as this. As Bledsoe and Robey show, in an ethnography of literacy that eschews many of the misconceptions cited here, the form of letters in Sierra Leone is itself part of their message: the fact of writing down a message that could, functionally speaking, be as easily transmitted orally, signifies the status of the recipient, although this may be balanced by the colour of the ink used, red for instance signifying lack of respect (Bledsoe and Robey, 1985). In our own society, similarly, the status associations of written forms can lend added power to documents and letters over oral communication (Williams, 1976). Such significance cannot, in fact, be detached from the supposed intrinsic 'meanings' of words communicated; the whole social practice, including the form of literacy, serves to constitute meaning. To dismiss the Tangu representation as a 'failure to perceive anomaly' does not do justice to the full significance of Tangu uses of literacy, to judge from what we know of literacy from other contexts. What it does do, of course, is to reinforce the distinction that is central to the popular model of literacy, between 'logical' and 'socially embedded' uses, described here as respectively 'secular' and 'ritualized'. In terms of the 'secular' model, native practices of literacy are represented as illogical and mistaken.

These points are brought out more fully by a further analysis of Meggitt's interpretation of this material. He sees Burridge's example and others derived from his own work as indicating a native view of literacy which means that 'European-sponsored education has little objective value for the majority of the people' (Meggitt, 1968, p. 304). What he means by 'objective' is brought out in his distinction between the 'cargo cults' of coastal Melanesia and the more pragmatic movements found in the highlands and in, for instance, the Paliau Movement among the Manus of the Admiralty islands.

Following the retreat from the Europeans, when local peoples realized they were not receiving any of the wealth and status they had expected, Meggitt sees a return to 'traditional modes of communicating with the supernatural': 'Seances, dream interpretation, vision inducement and similar equivocal techniques were again practised in endeavours to learn the whereabouts of the cargo and how to bring it to the people'. It is within this context that he views the uses of literacy within cargo cults: 'in addition the ritualized manipulation of writing (for instance in objectively irrelevant letters and books – objets trouvés', as it were) continued to be regarded as an equally potent device for understanding supernatural events and motives' (Meggit, 1968, p. 303).

This kind of cargo activity Meggitt opposes to that exhibited by the Paliau Movement. Paliau earns Meggitt's praise because he tries to persuade his 'ignorant' followers that hard-work and other such European virtues are the secret of wealth, not the kinds of symbolic resistance to colonialism represented by 'cargo cults'. The cults, then, are marginalized as 'mystical', their ideological significance underplayed and this is supposedly brought home by their use of a kind of literacy that has no 'objective' value. He sees Paliau as typical of a category of 'farseeing men' who attempted 'to devise a political and economic movement for change, in which writing regains its typically European secular status as a means of communication'. Again, then, European uses of literacy are represented as simply straightforward and rational, with no ambiguity, 'equivocation' or manipulation and representing 'objective' value. Recent critiques of the 'autonomous' model of literacy have demonstrated that literacy is not so simply described, that European uses are as varied and ambiguous as any other (Heath, 1983; Stubbs, 1980; Barton and Ivanic, 1991). The notion that writing represents simply the full and unambiguous meaning of the words cited is recognized as an unhelpful reification, unrelated to actual social practice. The representation of words in written form, within letters and books, is not 'objectively irrelevant' and attention to their form is not to be so lightly dismissed as trivial concern for 'objets trouvés'. Part of their meaning stems from the form in which they are embedded and this is a feature of literacy practice in general, whether in the academic's study or within cargo movements. In linguistic terms, part of the meaning of written channels of communication lies in paralinguistic and pragmatic features of their production as well as in the more obvious syntactical and lexical meanings on which linguists have traditionally concentrated. Melanesian emphasis on the form, then, is not so simpleminded or unusual as Meggitt believes. The use of documents in terms of their external appearance, deriving status from their formal appearance, decoration, covers etc., as well as making use of the 'words on the page' is a familiar and frequent feature of the ideological character of literacy. As Clanchy has demonstrated with reference to the importation of certain literacy practices by the Normans in eleventh-century England, the shift from memory to written record involves shifts in the social conventions associated with uses of reading and writing, in learning to trust certain forms of documentation rather than others and in the significance attributed to their external form as well as to content. If, then, we look at Fijian uses of literacy in 'cargo cults' from the point of view of the context and form of literacy practice, rather than simply the content, we can see that the Fijians were appropriately employing features of literacy that the missionaries had themselves applied to their own uses of the medium: the use of form to indicate meaning; the use of the status of written texts to manipulate readers; the play on ambiguity to reinforce the writer's position in a power structure. The anthropologists, then, are obscuring the comparison when they criticize these practices as fundamentally different from 'proper' European uses of literacy.

Manipulation

Meggitt, for instance, argues that for Melanesians 'the virtue of writing lay in men's ability to manipulate it as an entity in a defined ritual fashion'. For him and for Clammer, such uses of literacy in cargo cults represent mistaken perceptions by the natives of the true nature of literacy. The Fijians are embedded in supernatural beliefs and so mistake the 'straightforward technique of secular action' that literacy really is. From the perspective of the ideological model of literacy, however, the native perception of literacy is by no means so naive and mystical as Clammer and Meggitt would have us believe. In the Fijian case, the specific uses of literacy that were being taught to the natives by European missionaries were themselves embedded in an ideology that entailed just such 'manipulation' of literacy in defined 'ritual' fashion. In the mission schools texts were limited, reading was emphasized rather than writing, writing materials were scarcely available, while teaching techniques involved chanting, repetition and copying with little attempt 'to convey meaning to the mind of the student'. All of this experience provided the Fijians with a model of literacy in which manipulation and ritual were paramount. It was, then, an appropriate use of the political potential of literacy for them to apply it in this way themselves. Having been subject to the process themselves they tried to manipulate it in the same way as the Europeans in order to establish their own authority and political position.

If their aim is represented as 'to get a grip on the missionary God and force from him his secrets' then it can be interpreted, in less patronizing terms, as attempting to get a grip on the mission goods and force from the missionaries the secrets of their wealth and power. In these efforts they were, in fact, quite right to recognize that literacy was closely connected with such wealth and power. If they wanted the latter they had to command the former and the Europeans had shown them one way to do so.

'Ambiguity'

Even with regard to native interpretation of the content of literacy, we would do well to resist the easy scorn generated by the 'autonomous' approach, which assumes that only 'unambigous meaning' is worthy of serious intellectual attention. Members of the cults were, in fact, quite justified in taking writing as an 'inherently ambiguous mode of communication': this is what it is in most social contexts, and certainly in nineteenth-century Melanesia where the missionaries made full use of its ambiguity to maintain their own position. The meaning communicated in the case of the writing on the 'chip', for instance, in the example cited earlier was intended to be quite different for the European missionary than it was for the native chief. For the mission-ary's wife it was meant to represent an order with which, in view of her relationship to the writer, she was willing to comply. For the chief its meaning was mystified and made awesome, as part of the political control of local populations by the Europeans. Maintaining that awe and mystery, while teaching enough literacy to convert sufficient locals to carry out necessary bureaucratic duties as public servants, was an essential part of the European use of literacy in nineteenth- and twentieth-century Melanesia. That use hinged on its ambiguity. That the meaning of a text and of literacy itself could be different for European colonists than it was for their subjects, was the key to political control. The representation of literacy as unam-biguous that we find in European ideology can be interpreted as a form of political disguise of its true nature in order to privilege European interpretations and maintain European hegemony. The anthropologists appear to have taken this representation at its face value. In their claims that writing is essentially 'unambiguous' they reveal how little they have questioned its uses in their own culture.

The cults can, then, be interpreted as political acts employing apt symbols and making realistic political use of literacy practices. For Melanesians to have rejected such uses and to have simply learnt in schools what was represented as the 'technical', 'neutral', 'straightfor-ward', 'unambiguous' aspects of literacy would have been to miss important aspects of literacy – in this case the significance of form, manipulation and ambiguity – that related directly to the continua-tion of European power in their countries. This, of course, was what the Europeans wanted and their continued representation of literacy as a simple technical skill aptly fulfilled their own political purposes. Their scorn of the cults' experiments with literacy practice and with the social institutions that had accompanied its development serve ideologically to direct attention away from these politically vital aspects of literacy and towards safer, politically neutralized aspects that could be used to support the *status quo*. Acceptance of the 'technical' model of literacy by the indigenous populations would, then, have been already an acceptance of aspects of European ideo-logy; it would have conceded a monopoly of 'logic' and 'rationality' to European ways of thinking and to the institutional forms in which they have developed. It would also have avoided any challenge to the

European monopoly of the technology of literacy, the presses, newspapers, school text books etc. In these ways indoctrination with the 'technical' model of literacy can be a way of maintaining the *status quo* and restricting the arena in which 'political' protest is held to be legitimate. To raise political questions in the context of literacy teaching can be ruled out as inappropriate, if it can be maintained that such teaching is simply at a technical, functional level.

The cults' continuing emphases, to the contrary, on the social nature of literacy and the political and ideological implications of the institutions in which it was conveyed and used, represented in itself a challenge to this European hegemony. It kept the political issues on the agenda in contexts from which the Europeans were trying to rule it out — notably the bureaucracy, collection of records, control of finances etc. If we read the account of the cults' practices in this light we find that their obsession with literacy is more appropriate and 'rational' than Clammer and others would have us believe. The emphasis would not be whether the cults achieved immediate 'success' or can be shown to be 'instrumental' or not, but rather, on their significance at an ideological level. At this level they can be interpreted as confronting the sources of European power, such as control of the means of communication and as exploring how such control relates to political and economic control. They experiment, as it were, with the language, the methodologies and the institutional forms in which the relationship of ideology and power is manifest. They thus help people to become practised in their own independent uses of literacy and to develop it for themselves rather than always practising it passively under European control and supervision. In broader terms, they represent transformations of European discourses on literacy and education into local discourse, language and ideology (cf. Asad, 1980; Parkin, 1985). Within this framework it may well be appropriate to attempt to imagine how, 'If I were a Melanesian', I would respond to European domination. Using that approach in this way might, for instance, lead us to recognize elements of local discourse in the early descriptions of Melanesian acquaintance with literacy, as in the case where the chief appropriates a 'chip' and communicates its power to his followers, and where students set about constructing their own materials with which to write and to record 'the principal portions of every discourse they heard'. Cargo cults can be interpreted as more fully developed and institutionalized forms of these early independent practices. European scorn of the chief with his 'chip' and of the students with their home-made pens and slates, was as misplaced and short-sighted as was their scorn of cargo cults at a later period.

That scorn still pervades some of the anthropological accounts of literacy acquisition and use and of cargo-cult phenomena. I would argue that one reason for its persistence in writers who have otherwise attempted to eschew colonial and ethnocentric judgements, is that the anthropologists have accepted uncritically those theories about literacy that I have described above in terms of the 'autonomous' model. While clarifying to some extent the theoretical foundations for their descriptions of non-European religion and belief, they have left largely untheorized their representation of the uses and consequences of literacy. Consequently, not only do their analyses of literacy practices themselves suffer, but also that of those more general changes which accompany literacy, such as, in the Melanesian case, cargo cults.

Since in future much of the description of literacy practice is going to have to be conducted in such a cross-cultural perspective and, as in the Melanesian case, in terms of social change and the encounters between very different cultures, then it is important that the dangers implicit in such studies are made explicit. By highlighting the misconceptions that arise from the use of the 'autonomous' model of literacy and the 'if I were a horse' procedures associated with it, we can, I hope, move some way towards providing a theoretical and methodological framework for the study of literacy and orality in their social contexts. It is within this framework, I believe, that questions regarding the shift from orality to literacy and back can best be answered.

References

Anderson, C.A. (1966) 'Literacy and Schooling on the Threshold: Some Historical Cases', in C.A. Anderson and M. Bowman (eds) *Education and Economic Development*. Frank Cass: London.

Asad, T. (1980) 'Anthropology and the Analysis of Ideology', *Man*, n.s., vol. 14, no. 4.

Barton, and Ivanic, R. (eds) (1991) *Literacy in the Community*. Sage: London.

Bledsoe, C. and Robey, K. (1985) 'Arabic Literacy and Secrecy among the Mende of Sierra Leone', *Man*, n.s., vol. 21, no. 2: 202–26.

Bloch, M. (1989) 'Literacy and Enlightenment', in K. Schousboe and M.T. Larsen (eds) *Literacy and Society*. Akademsig Forlag: Copenhagen, pp. 15–38.

Bloomfield, I. (1933) *Language*. Henry Holt: New York.

Burridge, K. (1960) *Mambu: a Melanesian Millenium*. Methuen: London.

Clammer, J. (1976) *Literacy and Social Change: a Case Study of Fiji*. Brill: Leiden.

Clammer, J. (1980) 'Towards an Anthropology of Literacy: the Effects of Mass Literacy on Language Use and Social Organisation', in *Language Forum*, vol. 4, no. 3.

Clanchy, M. (1979) *From Memory to Written Record: England 1066–1307*. Edward Arnold: London.

Cole, M. and Scribner, S. (1981) *The Psychology of Literacy*, Harvard UP: Cambridge, Massachusetts.

Donald, J. (1981) 'Language, Literacy and Schooling', Open University course no. U203, *Popular Culture*.

Evans-Pritchard, E.E. (1970) 'Lévy-Bruhl's Theory of Primitive Mentality', *Journal of the Anthropological Society of Oxford*, vol. 1, no. 2.

Finnegan, R. (1973) 'Literacy Versus Non-literacy: the Great Divide', in R. Finnegan and R. Horton (eds) *Modes of Thought*. Faber: London.

Finnegan, R. (1979) 'Attitudes to Speech and Language among the Limba of Sierra Leone', *Odu*, n.s., no. 2.

Finnegan, R. (1988) *Literacy and Orality*. Blackwell: Oxford.

Frazer, J.G. (1890) *The Golden Bough*. Macmillan: London.

Furet, F. and Ozouf, J. (1982) *Reading and Writing: Literacy in France from Calvin to Jules Ferry*. CUP: Cambridge.

Goelman, H., Oberg, A. and Smith, F. (eds) (1983) *Awakening to Literacy*. Heinemann: New York.

Golden, H. (1965) 'Literacy and Social Change in Underdeveloped Countries', *Rural Sociology*, vol. 20.

Goody, J. (1968) *Literacy in Traditional Societies*. CUP: Cambridge.

Goody, J. (1977) *The Domestication of the Savage Mind*. CUP: Cambridge.

Goody, J. and Cole, M. (1977) 'Writing and Formal Operations: a Case Study among the Vai', *Africa*, vol. 47, no. 3.

Graff, H.J. (1979) *The Literacy Myth: Literacy and Social Structure in the Nineteenth-Century City*. Academic Press: London.

Graff, H.J. (1982) *Literacy and Social Development in the West: a Reader*. CUP: Cambridge.

Hamilton, D. and Barton, M. (1985) 'Social and Cognitive Factors in the Development of Writing', in A. Lock and C. Peters (eds) *The Handbook of Human Symbolic Evolution*. OUP: Oxford.

Heath, S.B. (1980) 'The Function and Uses of Literacy', *Journal of Communication*, no. 30.

Heath, S.B. (1982) 'What No Bedtime Story Means: Narrative Skills at Home and School', *Language in Society*, vol. 11.

Heath, S.B. (1983) *Ways with Words*. CUP: Cambridge.

Henderson, G.C. (1931) *Fiji and the Fijians 1835–6*. Angus and Robertson: Sydney.

Hymes, D. (ed.) (1964) *Language in Culture and Society*. Harper: New York.

Hymes, D. and Fought, J. (1975) *American Structuralism*. Mouton: New York.

Levine, K. (1980) *Becoming Literate: Final Report on a Research Project 'Adult Illiteracy and the Socialization of Adult Illiterates'*. SSRC: London.

Lévy-Bruhl, L. (1926) *How Natives Think*, translated by L.A. Clare. Blackwell: Oxford.

Lienhardt, R.G. (1964) *Social Anthropology*. OUP: Oxford.

Lienhardt, R.G. (1980) 'Self: Public and Private. Some African Representations', *Journal of the Anthropological Society of Oxford*, vol. XI, no. 2.

Manghubai, F. (1985a) 'Literacy in Multilingual, Multiethnic Small Island States' in D. Wagner (ed.) (1987) *The Future of Literacy in a Changing World*. Pergamon Press: Oxford.

Manghubai, F. (1985b) Personal Correspondence.

Meggitt, D. (1968) 'Uses of Literacy in New Guinea and Melanesia', in J. Goody (1968) *Literacy in Traditional Societies*. CUP: Cambridge.

Olson, D. (1977) 'From Utterance to Text: the Bias of Language in Speech and Writing', *Harvard Educational Review*, no. 47.

Ong, W. (1977) *Interfaces of the Word*. Cornell UP: Ithaca, New York.

Ong, W. (1982a) *Orality and Literacy*. Methuen: London.

Ong, W. (1982b) 'Literacy and Orality in Our Times', *Pacific Quarterly Moana*, vol. 7, no. 2.

Oxenham, J. (1980) *Literacy: Writing, Reading and Social Organization*. Routledge: London.

Parkin, D. (1985) 'Political Language', *Annual Review of Anthropology*, vol. 13.

Parry, J. (1989) 'The Brahmanical Tradition and the Technology of the Intellect', in K. Schousboe and M.T. Larsen (eds) *Literacy and Society*. Akademsig Forlag: Copenhagen.

Reder, S. and Green, K. (1983) 'Contrasting Patterns of Literacy in an Alaskan Fishing Village', in D. Wagner. (ed.) *The Future of Literacy in a Changing World*. Pergamon Press: Oxford.

Schieffelin, B. and Gilmore, P. (eds) (1986) *The Acquisition of Literacy: Ethnographic Perspectives*. Ablex: Norwood, New Jersey.

Shuman, A. (1986) *Storytelling Rights: The Uses of Oral and Written Texts by Urban Adolescents*. CUP: Cambridge.

Skorupski, J. (1976) *Symbol and Theory*. CUP: Cambridge.

Street, B.V. (1975a) *The Savage in Literature*. Routledge: London.

Street, B.V. (1975b) 'The *Mullāh*, the *Shahnameh* and the *Madrasseh*: Some Aspects of Literacy in Iran', *Asian Affairs*, vol. 62.

Street, B.V. (1982–) 'Literacy and Ideology', in *Red Letters*, Vol. 12.

Street, B.V. (1983) 'Literacy Campaigns in UK', in *Literature, Teaching Politics*, vol. 2. Sussex University.

Street, B.V. (1984) *Literacy in Theory and Practice*. CUP: Cambridge.

Stubbs, M. (1980) *Language and Literacy: The Sociolinguistics Of Reading and Writing*. RKP: London.

Wagner, D. (ed.), (1983) *Literacy and Ethnicity*, vol. 42. *International Journal of Sociology of Language*. Mouton: New York.

Wagner, D. (ed.) (1987) *The Future of Literacy in a Changing World*. Pergamon Press: Oxford.

Wagner, D., Messick, B. and Spratt, J. (1986) 'Studying Literacy in Morocco', in B. Schieffelin and P. Gilmore (eds) *The Acquisition of Literacy*. Ablex: Norwood, New Jersey.

Wilson, B. (ed.) (1974) *Rationality*. Blackwell: Oxford.

Williams, J. (1837) *A Narrative of Missionary Enterprises in the South Sea Islands*. London.

Williams, R. (1976) *Human Communication*. Penguin: Harmondsworth.

Worsley, P. (1976) *The Trumpet Shall Sound*. Weidenfeld and Nicolson: London.

Section 3:

Literacy in Education

Introduction

The third Section builds on the case studies and the conceptual tools developed in earlier Sections, in the context of education in industrialized societies. I attempt to test out some of the earlier ideas and methods in relation to schooled practice. Ethnographic approaches to the study of language in education have, of course, been popular for some time, especially in the USA, but their application to literacy practices is more recent, and their value in the broader context of educational policy is only recently being recognized, as it is in relation to development policy.

Chapter 5: The Schooling of Literacy

Within the larger framework set out above, this chapter provides a specific case study of literacy-in-practice in particular homes and classrooms in the USA. This piece was researched and written jointly with Joanna Street, for whose permission to use the collective voice here I am grateful. Addressing the question of why one particular variety of literacy among many comes to be seen and reproduced as the standard, we suggest that a major way in which schooled literacy is asserted, for parents and teachers alike, is through the establishment of a link between literacy and pedagogy. We hypothesize that, by means of this linkage, literacy itself comes to be viewed and practised within a framework of learning, teaching and schooling. This variety thus acquires authority in relation to the many other practices with which literacy has been and could be identified. By means of ethnographic enquiry in homes and schools in a middle-class suburb of a north-eastern American city, we attempted to examine the relationship between ideas about and uses of literacy in the community and in the school.

It has been assumed in much of the educational literature that middle-class homes are closely aligned with school practice and ideas regarding literacy. Shirley Brice Heath, for instance, while providing detailed accounts of white and black working-class homes in her classic *Ways with Words* (Heath, 1983), offered little ethnographic detail on middle-class, 'mainstream' family life. The present research was intended to fill that gap in the literature and to consider whether there might not be differences between the ideas about literacy that are held in schools and that underpin school pedagogy and the actual uses and views of literacy in the children's homes. Tape recordings were made of parents reading with their children: parents were asked to keep a 'Literacy Diary' (a methodological tool now being applied by other researchers), recording literacy events in the home in the sequence in which they occurred and commenting upon what counts as literacy according to different family members; and interviews were held with parents and tape-recorded regarding their literacy diaries and their ideas about literacy as it related to their children. Similarly, tape recordings were made of the classrooms that the same children attended and interviews were held with their teachers. Initial findings suggest that schools spend considerable time on what Bloome, Puro and Theodorou (1989) call 'procedural display', in which children are taught the procedures and authority associated with schooled literacy, while in the home there may be other varieties of literacy practice than those associated with school, but these may be undervalued or referred to shamefully as improper literacy. On the other hand, the expected 'gap' between home and schooled literacy was not apparent in this context. We speculate that the degree of congruence between home and school identified here may be a result not so much of school influencing home as of general middle-class values (including entrepreneurship, hard work, etc.) affecting both contexts. Further empirical work along these lines might help link the new literacy theories with particular practices in home and school: until then, we have to be wary of generalization, although some account of the link between literacy and pedagogy is emerging.

Chapter 6: The Implications of the New Literacy Studies for Pedagogy

This chapter attempts to develop some of the implications of the theoretical positions outlined in the papers collected here for the practice and policy of education. While wary of claiming too much from the position mainly of a researcher, it does seem to me incumbent on those of us who argue for new theoretical and methodological approaches to literacy to make some attempt to follow this through into the educational process itself. I also use the opportunity to summarize and update those aspects of the ideological model of literacy that are significant in this context. I consider again the notion of literacy events and the ways in which 'literacy practices' can be employed as a more encompassing term that allows us to recognize the models and concepts of literacy that actors themselves bring to the events. I consider the problems with the culturalist as opposed to the ideological model of literacy and also address the difficulties that have arisen with the concept of multiple literacies – a concept that I believe is crucial in challenging the autonomous model, but which is beginning to be discredited as each observer offers their own criteria for different literacies and as metaphors and extensions of the term move further and further away from the social practices of reading and writing. I then consider the implications of the ideological model of literacy for a number of areas of educational debate in recent years, from different parts of the political spectrum. I conclude that this requires teachers and educational planners to assist learners to understand the critical principles that underlie both their literacy practices and the pedagogical practices through which they have learnt them.

5 The Schooling of Literacy

(With J. Street)

Previous chapters have established the ideological and cultural nature of literacy practices. In this chapter I develop the argument with respect to a case study of particular classrooms and communities in the USA and relate them to the wider debates in that country regarding 'cultural literacy' (Hirsch, 1987; Bloom, 1987). The chapter was originally written in collaboration with J. Street, and I continue to use the pronominal plural to indicate the shared nature of the research. The question that concerned us was: if, as we argue, there are multiple literacies, how is that one particular variety has come to be taken as the only literacy? Among all of the different literacies practised in the community, the home, and the workplace, how is it that the variety associated with schooling has come to be the defining type, not only to set the standard for other varieties but to marginalize them, to rule them off the agenda of literacy debate? Non-school literacies have come to be seen as inferior attempts at the real thing, to be compensated for by enhanced schooling.

We are interested in exploring the ways in which, both at home and at school, dominant conceptions of literacy are constructed and reproduced in such a way as to marginalize alternatives and, we would suggest, to control key aspects of language and thought. We hypothesize that the mechanism through which meanings and uses of 'literacy' take on this role is the 'pedogogization' of literacy. By this we mean that literacy has become associated with educational notions of Teaching and Learning and with what teachers and pupils do in schools, at the expense of the many other uses and meanings of literacy evident from the comparative ethnographic literature. We use *pedagogy* not in the narrow sense of specific skills and tricks of the trade used by teachers but in the broader sense of institutionalized processes of teaching and learning, usually associated with the school but increasingly identified in home practices associated with reading and writing. Whether we are observing parent–child interactions, the development of educational toys and 'software' in the home, or the procedures associated with classroom learning, *pedagogy* in this sense has taken on the character of an ideological force controlling social relations in general and conceptions of reading and writing in particular.

The chapter is organized around a number of key theoretical concepts, informed by some illustrative data from field-work undertaken in the USA during 1988. We begin with an analysis of what we mean by the 'pedagogization' of literacy, highlighting the cultural specificity of this form with reference to comparative material from social situations in which literacy is not associated with schooling or pedagogy. We then briefly describe the school and community from which we draw some illustrative data; we consider in this context some of the processes of pedagogization, such as the objectification of language, metalinguistic usages, space labelling, and classroom procedure. After having suggested some of the ways of studying *how* the schooling of literacy is effected, we conclude with some suggestions as to *why* this form of literacy has acquired such importance in contemporary society, focusing on the relationship between literacy, ideology, and nationalism. Finally, we draw some conclusions regarding possible directions for future research.

Literacy without schooling

We begin by establishing what is meant by the notion of different 'literacies' and of conceptualizing literacy outside schooling and pedagogy. Literacy is so embedded within these institutions in contemporary society that it is sometimes difficult for us to disengage and recognize that, for most of history and in great sections of contemporary society, literacy practices remain embedded in other social institutions. While Ogbu's definition of *literacy* as 'synonymous with academic performance', 'the ability to read and write and compute in the form taught and expected in formal education' (Ogbu, 1990), would probably receive general agreement in contemporary society, it is put into perspective by a recent account by Reid (1988, p. 218) of literacy in pre-sixteenth-century South-East Asia:

> The old Indonesian ka-ga-nga alphabet ... was taught in no school and had no value either vocationally or in reading any established or secular literature. The explanation for its persistence was the local custom of *manjan*, a courting game whereby young men and women would gather in the evenings and the youths would fling suggestive quatrains written in the old script to the young women they fancied.

Many cultures in this region adopted writing systems originally introduced from India, and 'women took up writing as actively as men, to use in exchanging notes and recording debts and other female matters which were in the domestic domain' (Reid, 1988, p. 218). With the arrival of Islam and Christianity in the sixteenth century, however, 'a more restricted, male-based literacy drove out the old script' and a pattern emerged that is common in the contemporary world as western influence spreads: 'a curious paradox that the growth of written culture probably reduced the number of people who could write by associating writing with the sacral and the solemn' and with male uses of literacy. The widespread use of literacy by women, in non-educational contexts prior to the introduction of western schooled literacy, is becoming attested for a range of times and places: Yin-Yee Ko (1989), for instance, describes how, in seventeenth-century China, educated middle-class women wrote poetry as a means of constructing a private female culture against the homogenizing male character of late Imperial Chinese culture. Mickulecky (1985, p. 2) records the uses of literacy by women from the rising gentry in fifteenth-century England to write letters 'concerned with business affairs of the family, personal intrigues, duty and death'. The accounts of literacy in contemporary Lancaster, England (Barton and Ivanic, 1991), show women using 'community' literacy in mediating with outside agencies such as social services. Rockhill (1987) describes how Hispanic women's uses of literacy to manage the home in Los Angeles were invisible to a community that identified literacy with male employment and schooling: these 'illiterate' women had then to attend classes to acquire 'proper' literacy, that is the reading and writing skills and conventions associated with schooling that can be tested through formal mechanisms (Rockhill, 1987). The invisibility of women's literacy (along with much of their social activity) is a product not only of patriarchal society but also of dominant definitions and concepts of literacy.

As we saw in Section 1, the literacies of non-European peoples have generally been ignored by developers bringing western institutions and schooling to different parts of the world. Only recently has it been recognized that many writing systems have been developed outside of the western context, the best known being those of the Vai (Scribner and Cole, 1981) and Mende (Bledsoe and Robey, 1986) in West Africa and of the Apache and Cherokee among native North Americans (Harbsmeier, 1989). More significant for the current argument has been the variety of 'literacies' that are being documented by ethnographers, in which a script brought by outsiders such as missionaries or teachers has been 'taken hold of' by local people (Kulick and Stroud, 1993) and adapted to indigenous meanings and uses. In the village in New Guinea that Kulick and Stroud studied, missionary literacy was incorporated into local conventions of language use rather than being used for the purposes intended by teachers. Skills developed in speech making, involving the avoidance of self-assertion or of putting others down, were also prominent in the ways that letters came to be written. As literacy is added to the rich communicative repertoire that already exists in the receiving societies, they adapt and amend it to local meanings, concepts of identity, and epistemologies: as Kulick and Stroud express it, the question is not what 'impact' literacy has on people but how people affect literacy. Besnier's (1989) account of how the people of the Pacific atoll of Nukulaelae took hold of missionary literacy, shows how, whereas, in New Guinea literacy was absorbed into pre-existing communicative conventions, on Nukulaelae it was used to add a genre to the communicative repertoire. In speech, it was conventionally improper to express affect, while the new literacy gave scope for its full expression, particularly in letters. This suggests a further challenge to dominant assumptions about literacy in which speech is usually associated with self-expression, feeling, and subjectivity while writing is conventionally associated with detachment, objectivity, and 'scientific' discourse (Tannen, 1985), an argument discussed above in the Introduction and dealt with in more detail below in chapter 7. The Nukulaelae material, along with that from many other parts of the world, brings home how far the associations commonly made with literacy are in fact cultural conventions rather than products of the medium itself. The uses of literacy by women; its association with informal, non-religious, and non-bureaucratic practices; its affective and expressive functions; and the incorporation of oral conventions into written usage – all are features of literacy practice that have tended to be marginalized or destroyed by modern, western literacy with its emphasis on formal, male, and schooled aspects of communication. Much, then, of what goes with schooled literacy turns out to be the product of western assumptions about schooling, power, and knowledge rather than being necessarily intrinsic to literacy itself. The role played by developmental perspectives in schooling, for instance, means that the acquisition of literacy becomes isomorphic with the child's development of specific social identities and positions: their power in society becomes associated with the kind and level of literacy they have acquired.

These examples of the relationship of variations in literacy to relative power and knowledge are not confined to the 'Third World' or to technologically simpler societies: recent ethnographies of literacy in the USA provide similar evidence of the rich varieties of literacy outside of school and formal learning processes and their significance for people's identities and positions in society. Weinstein-Shr (1993), for instance, compares Hmong refugees in Philadelphia in terms of their literacy practices and discovers two quite different sets of meanings and uses. One man, Chou Chang, learned standard schooled literacy in an evening class and used this to be a 'gate-keeper' for his community, mediating with agencies such as social services. Pao Youa, however, dropped out of the literacy class and appeared to 'fail' in dominant terms. However, Weinstein-Shr came across him some time later in a position of considerable authority that was largely legitimated through his uses of literacy: he kept scrapbooks of cuttings and pictures from newspapers, magazines, and letters that mentioned the Hmong and that represented an authoritative 'history' of his people in recent circumstances. Members of the community would go to him as to a man of knowledge, and he would call upon the corpus of written material he had collected to discuss and determine key issues of community identity. The literacy with which he was dealing had nothing to do with formal schooling or pedagogy, and indeed it is likely that he could not formally decode the phonemic signs in all of the materials with which he was surrounded; but his literacy played a significant role in local politics and identity and in establishing his authority in the community (see also Camitta, 1993; Shuman, 1983).

Similarly, Fishman's (1991) account of Amish literacy demonstrates the close association of literacy practices with identity, authority, and concepts of knowledge that are not necessarily those of schooled literacy. When she arrived in the community, she asked the girls of the family she was staying with to keep 'dialogue journals' as a way of observing their literacy practices and establishing communication with them. But they refused, and it later became obvious that their conceptions of literacy were at variance with those that underlie the use of such journals. Amish communicative conventions require an 'other-centredness' that involves downplaying the self and focusing on the community. As in the New Guinea case, self-assertiveness was considered improper, and this became reflected in written conventions as these were added to the communicative repertoire: for the Amish girls to write of their own experience and feelings would be wrong – a challenge to Amish conceptions of identity and knowledge. The conventions associated with current writing practices and pedagogy in American schooling are not simply matters of technique and of neutral learning skills but may be associated with deep levels of cultural meaning and belief: other literacies exist alongside the dominant, school-oriented versions.

Also in the USA, Arlene Fingeret has shown how the kind of community literacies described above may mean that literacy and other skills become reciprocal parts of an exchange process, thus obviating the need for each individual to develop each skill to a high degree. A person without highly developed literacy skills may complete all of the literacy tasks required of him or her in modern urban America by passing the tasks of filling out forms, writing letters, and the like on to another member of the community in exchange for, say, skills at mending car engines or managing transport arrangements. Within such community networks, there is no more stigma attached to lacking reading and writing skills than there is to lacking the skills of the motor mechanic (Fingeret, 1983). Similar findings occur in work from Mexico (King, 1994), the UK (Street, 1988), Somalia (Lewis, 1986), and many other parts of the world.

Literacy, then, need not be associated with schooling or with pedagogy: Ogbu's definition with which we began is inappropriate if we are to understand the full and rich meanings of literacy practices in contemporary society. Research needs, instead, to begin from a more comparative, more ethnographically based conception of literacy as the *social* practices of reading and writing and to eschew value judgements about the relative superiority of schooled literacy over other literacies.

Literacy in the community and in the school

While mainly concerned with exploring, these issues at a theoretical level, we suggest how they might be developed empirically by reference to a small, pilot research project we conducted on home and school literacy practices in a community in the USA (a full research programme is planned for the future). Just as we wish to eschew culturally biased judgement of different literacies in different communities, so we wish to avoid making judgements on schooled literacy. We are not concerned with evaluating the practices we describe below but with analyzing them ethnographically as social phenomena. The peculiar practices associated with literacy in schools and, increasingly, in the home and community in much of late-twentieth-century American society represent a fascinating and important addition to the complex and varied repertoire of literacy practices across both time and space that ethnographers and historians are now beginning to reveal. Why and how this particular version of literacy practices is reproduced and sustained in contemporary society is a theoretical and ethnographic question – crucially bound up with issues of power in the wider society – rather than a matter of educational evaluation. While Cook-Gumperz (1986), Soltow and Stevens (1981), and Howard (1991) have amply documented the historical processes by which 'schooled' literacy has become the dominant mode over the last century, the comparative questions their work poses have less often been applied to the current situation itself and to the reproduction of that dominance. It is within this framework that we developed a small pilot project to attempt to work out how such research might be framed and conducted. The material presented here is not sufficiently full or detailed to merit the term *ethnography*; rather, we see it as contributing towards future research of an ethnographic kind in this area.

The school on which we focused was set in an upper-middle-class suburb of a major American city that suffered from gross poverty, social inequality and inner-city decline. Many of those who lived in this suburb had fled there to avoid these problems. The school was one of the few state schools that enjoyed a high reputation in middle-class and professional circles, and many families made considerable financial efforts to buy themselves into the area. House prices were high, and, in most families, both partners were obliged to work to meet mortgage costs and so on. They would frequently leave for work in the city early in the morning, leaving their children at the day-care centre at the school and returning in the evening to pick the children up from the centre, which remained open well after school closing time. The school had classes from first grade through to fifth with about twenty pupils per class and two or three classes in each year. We observed and taped classroom practices, in the first and fifth grades, each of us spending three mornings or afternoons in each class. We also taped discussion sessions with each of the teachers in which we asked about their conceptions of literacy. Outside of the school, we conducted interviews with half a dozen parents of children who attended the school and the classes we were observing, asked them to keep a 'Literacy Diary' by recording literacy events in their homes, and asked some families to tape-record the speech around these events. This focus upon literacy in middle-class, suburban homes is an aspect of literacy in the 'community' that has not received much research attention. Shirley Brice Heath's *Ways with Words* (1983), for instance, makes reference to it but she does not research it in any detail, appearing to assume that we all know what middle-class life and literacy are like.

We began the project by assuming a distinction between literacy practices in the community and in the school. We wanted to explore the ways in which the particular variety of literacy that we labelled 'school literacy' comes to dominate other forms of literacy in contemporary society. Our experience forced us to refine these ideas, particularly those regarding home and school literacies, and to recognize that the extent of similarity between practices of literacy in the community, in the home, and in the school make our earlier dichotomy unhelpful. Underlying literacy in all of these contexts is a common thread, derived from wider cultural and ideological processes. We focus here on one particular aspect of this common thread, the processes of pedagogization.

Processes of pedagogization

We found that one way of answering our questions about the pedagogization of literacy was to break it down into a number of specific processes and then to examine these processes in both home and school. In this chapter, we are particularly concerned with the processes that help construct an 'autonomous' model of literacy – in which many individuals, often against their own experience, come to conceptualize literacy as a separate, reified set of 'neutral' competencies, autonomous of social context – and with the procedures and social roles through which this model of literacy is disseminated and internalized.

The construction and internalization of the autonomous model of literacy is achieved by a number of means, some of which we will briefly attempt to illustrate from our data: the distancing of language from subjects – the ways in which language is treated as though it were a thing, distanced from both teacher and learner and imposing on them external rules and requirements as though they were but passive recipients; 'metalinguistic' usages – the ways in which the social processes of reading and writing are referred to and lexicalized within a pedagogic voice as though they were independent and neutral competencies rather than laden with significance for power relations and ideology; 'privileging' – the ways in which reading and writing are given status *vis-à-vis* oral discourse as though the medium were intrinsically superior and, therefore, those who acquired it would also become superior; and 'philosophy of language' – the setting of units and boundaries for elements of language use as though they were neutral, thereby disguising the ideological source of what are in fact social constructions, frequently associated with ideas about logic, order, scientific mentality, and so on.

Among the institutional processes that contribute to the construction and internalization of the pedagogic voice in school, we focus on 'space labelling' and 'procedures'. The institutionalization of a particular model of literacy operates not only through particular forms of speech and texts but in the physical and institutional space that is separated from 'everyday' space for purposes of teaching and learning and that derives from wider social and ideological constructions of the social and built world. 'Procedures' represent the way in which rules for the engagement of participants as teachers and learners are continuously asserted and reinforced within practices supposedly to do simply with using and talking about literacy: while apparently simply giving instructions about handling a text, for instance, teachers and parents are also embedding relations of hierarchy, authority and control.

A 'mix' of oral and literate media, sometimes referred to as an 'oral-literate' continuum, is to be observed in all of these processes: participants employ both oral and literate discursive strategies as they interact, in both home and school. But this interactive aspect of literacy and orality tends, within actual practice, to be disguised behind prescriptions and linguistic conventions that represent the linguistic modes as entirely separate, as though there were a 'great divide' between orality and literacy. This conception of literacy appears to be one of the major means whereby an autonomous model of literacy is internalized and disseminated in contemporary society. It is a conception endemic to pedagogized literacy.

Objectifying language

Much classroom discourse turns upon explicit attention to language and what it means for children. The contemporary literature on learning to read places great emphasis on the achievement of metalinguistic awareness and frequently presumes that the development of this highly valued ability is associated with the acquisition of literacy (Bruner, 1985; Teale and Sulzby, 1987; Wells, 1985; Wertsch, 1981). Self-awareness about language and the development of specific terms for describing it are seen as part of cognitive development, leading to critical thought, detachment, and objectivity, and it is taken as self-evident that the writing down of language facilitates these processes (Olson, Hildyard and Torrance, 1985). Given the powerful pressure in favour of this model of language within teacher training institutions in both the UK and the USA, it is not surprising to find it underpinning much classroom practice. However, while recognizing the significance of metalinguistic awareness, we would reject the claim that it is peculiarly associated with literacy and also question the tendency to focus on certain syntactic and formal features of language at the expense of other aspects as though language awareness were a matter of specific grammatical terminology.

Objectifying language at school

In the classroom we observed, teachers appeared to treat language as though it were something outside both the students and themselves, as though it had autonomous, non-social qualities that imposed themselves upon its users. The language of instruction presupposed and helped to construct distance between children and their language. Writing is one way of creating that distance – putting it on the blackboard serves as one technique for enabling children to see and objectify that process of learning. Once the language is on the board, on the worksheet, in the book, and so on, it becomes a separate problem for the teacher and children to work on together. In the sessions we observed, the teacher made an effort to get the children to identify with her as she worked out a problem in grammar or expression, as though they were commonly struggling against an outside authority to which they were both subject. The aim was to get children to follow her own work processes and mimic them. There was little discussion of the meaning of language, of alterative interpretations of texts, or of how the teacher arrived at her sense of what they meant. This was so even after library reading: views might be elicited before reading but responses were not called for afterwards. Similarly, book reports, in which students were asked to read a book and then present orally a structured report on it to the whole class, took on a ritualized and non-semantic character in which the aim appeared to be to develop schooled language rather than actually to discuss the books. In contexts such as these, it would seem, the final objective is to achieve mastery and authority over the text, whose meanings are not negotiable. Oral book reports are modelled on written language, as conceived within this subculture; planning, the use of topic sentences and paragraphing, and explicitness are carried over from how written language has been learned into spoken language. The school presentation of the text is, then, unproblematized regarding its meaning and content, focusing on form. Technical problems are set, to do with grammar and syntax, and solutions once given are assimilated to a general list of rules and prescriptions about the nature of language itself.

There were a number of ways in which this process operated collectively, so that the whole class was constructing a collective voice in ways that excluded exploration of the meanings of what was being uttered; the pledge of allegiance in which teacher and students chanted formulaic phrases together, certain question-and-answer sessions, some circle games. Similarly, diagnostic and evaluative tests were used as a way to create distance between the children and their own perception of their knowledge. The teacher identified with them and helped them through the process. This identification exacerbates the notion of the objective, neutral status of the text and reduces the role of speaker/reader to passive recipient rather than active negotiator of meaning. While the aims of language learning were spelled out in school documents as being based upon 'communication', the practice was frequently concerned with learning formalized uses of language and subjecting oral to written conventions.

Objectifying language at home

We observed similar processes in the children's homes, although they did not necessarily carry over directly from school as we at first imagined. Parents in middle-class homes are indeed frequently concerned about structuring learning for their children in the ways legitimized by the school (see Brooks, 1989). Similarly, from our observations, it appeared that attention to children's school exercises played a dominant part in everyday life: book reports, in particular, could take over the weekend as parents helped their child to spot 'topic sentences', develop links, and work up endings for their presentation to the class on Monday morning. Project work could take the whole family to the local library, which would be filled with teams of family researchers scanning encyclopedias and the non-fiction section for accounts of shells, electricity, fish, and so on. Acquisition of proper literacy was perceived as a 'problem' to be solved, a task to be accomplished: rules were set from outside and the child and parent were collaborators in responding to this hegemony. Tests were as much part of home practice as school.

From these practices, it at first appeared that home was simply dominated by school and that this would explain the pedagogization of literacy there. But the extent of the internalization of the pedagogic voice for literacy acquisition and dissemination suggests it is part of wider social and cultural currents. It is produced and reinforced through newspaper discussions on literacy, labelling on educational toys, political debates and parental discourses. In our interviews with parents of the children whose classes we observed, we found an ambivalence towards the school as an institution but a ready adoption of the pedagogized view of literacy that we identified there. These parents did not always see the school as the source of value and legitimacy in this area; they were developing their pedagogic voice from other sources too.

A number of parents had formed a Parent's Information Committee (PIC) to put pressure on the school where they thought it was failing to develop the appropriate model of literacy. At these meetings, it appeared that parents, not teachers, were the guardians of proper literacy. An example of this activity was parents pressuring school to adopt 'Writing Process' approaches: the PIC supported and lobbied for developments already taking place in the school district that involved in-service days on these ways of teaching literacy. Our findings suggest that the shift was not as radical as they believed because the same pedagogy underlay the focus on writing as process rather than as product. As Rudy (1989) demonstrated through research on Collaborative Learning of Writing in secondary classrooms in a nearby city, new approaches are frequently assimilated to traditional assumptions and ways of relating to students. We are not concerned here with evaluating these different approaches – collaborative, process-oriented writing instruction and traditional product-oriented writing instruction – but with demonstrating how both may be subsumed under the more general principle of the pedagogization of literacy. The reason the change from one to another is not always as significant as exponents of the different approaches would hope may be that they both persist in reducing reading and writing to particular social practices associated with 'learning', thereby missing the range of literacy practices associated with non-schooled purposes and concepts. In the classrooms we studied, the methods of teaching and learning associated with product-oriented teaching did not alter much as process approaches were introduced: literacy was still 'out there', an objective content to be taught through authority structures whereby pupils learned the proper roles and identities they were to carry into the wider world. Non-pedagogic literacies did not – indeed could not – figure in this process: the parents in the PIC were not trying to introduce alternative literacies to the school but simply to keep the teachers up to scratch in their pedagogic activities.

Similarly, in their own homes, the parents were claiming authority to direct their children's learning and thereby challenging the sole dominance of the school while at the same time marginalizing the alternative literacies that children may have encountered in the context of home, peer group and community in favour of a 'schooled' literacy. Homes were full of toys, games and videos that were explicitly directed towards school achievement and readiness, but the definition of that achievement became as much the property of the parent as the teacher. The labels in which these toys and the like were packaged, and the accompanying leaflets, used academic language, frequently derived from psychological literature, to legitimize and reinforce their educational value, and some of this language had crept into parents' discussions around literacy. It was within this discourse that they strove to keep the teachers up to scratch. Similarly, the project work on weekends was not simply subservient to school demands but used the school to create and reinforce home demands: children were learning to participate in the achievement culture that their parents saw as essential if they were to reproduce the parents' life-style and avoid the horrors of poverty of which the nearby city provided such stark evidence.

A perception of literacy as the major source of western supremacy, scientific achievement and so on, lay behind the willingness to engage in specific literacy tasks. An 'autonomous' model of literacy was thus crucial to the commitment parents showed, which they also expected of their children. Home interest in the use of tests, concern with formal features of literacy and language, the treatment of language as an external force with rules and requirements to be learned, and the intertwining of conventions associated with literacy and the management of texts with assertions of authority and control, including the organization of other people's time and space – all of these features of home literacy practice indeed complement the uses of literacy apparent in the children's school. The source, however, may not be the school itself but derived from larger cultural and ideological currents that influence both home and school. Just as in the Amish example (Fishman, 1991), it may be more fruitful to focus on continuities between home culture and school culture rather than on the discontinuities with which much of the research has been concerned. To do so, we argue, requires us to theorize literacy practices differently – to develop not only ethnographies of home and school but also ethnographies of literacy, of the kind advocated in this book.

Space labelling

In popular discourse, *the school* refers perhaps to the people who run or attend it, perhaps to the building in which it is situated that symbolizes its presence. But the school as an institution finds its main form of expression through a particular form of language, in evidence not only in the speech of teachers and the text of the written materials but in the classroom, on the walls, and in the stream of bureaucratic paperwork through which it constantly signifies and reproduces itself. The language of the teacher and of the text positions the subject (whether student or researcher), pins them to their seats, and locates them in a socially and authoritatively constructed space. How this space is constructed is crucial to our understanding of the particular linguistic and literacy processes with which this chapter is concerned.

The main building of the school we were investigating is large and square and breathes public importance. It is part of a whole genre of public architecture representing the state. Above the doorway in large letters, embedded in the wall, as part of the permanent structure, are the words X Elementary School. Inside the school, space is designated by authority and authority is expressed in signs: rooms are numbered and labelled, they have designated functions that are likewise labelled. The first notice one sees as one enters the building is 'All visitors must report to the office'. When one enters the building, one is situating oneself physically inside a particular universe of signs. Within a classroom, the pictures and notices on the walls continue this process of situating the individual within a sign system. This is particularly evident in the first-grade classroom. The children sit at the centre of a system of codes through which their experience is to be transformed. It is as though the walls themselves were a filtering screen through which the world outside the school is transformed and translated into various discrete sets of analytic concepts: lists of numbers, the letters of the alphabet, shapes and colours, lists of measurements – all the devices by which the experience of the senses can be filtered and then transformed into discrete social and analytic concepts, tabulated and measured. The five senses themselves dangle on separate little labels from a mobile. Time is filtered through a grid of days of the week, seasons, birthday charts and clock faces. The birthday chart situates the child herself within this catalogue of time, just as she is situated within space. The classroom's four walls are labelled 'south', 'east', 'north' and 'west', right and left hang on the wall – the room is framed as a signifying space with the child at the centre, making sense of things. These spatial categories only make sense when oriented to the child at the centre of the classroom, and they indicate in a very powerful way the contract between the individual and the institution that underpins the ideology of language within the school. This process of writing down and labelling experiences incorporates them into a visual system that is external to the child. The organization of the visual environment itself helps to construct and provide a model of the child's relationship to language and to the written word. The walls of the classroom become the walls of the world. The maps of the USA and the world on the wall at the front of the classroom indicate the system of signs through which that world may be attained.

Procedures

Procedures for organizing classroom time, work practices, and literacy materials dominate the classroom and form a major part of the pedagogic voice. One teacher told her students explicitly that they had to speak differently in class: 'Now you are in school, use your inside school voice'. Thereby school is separated from other times and places, and familiar everyday processes of speaking, reading and writing are given a distinct character and a special authority. A session is divided into phases by means of linguistic markers that have illocutionary force in actually constructing the separate times and spaces (but compare with Collins, 1993). The teacher continually interrupts students' work with statements about where the class are in her time frame and what to do next: 'Journals now: write how the group work went'; 'close your scripts up, all the pages inside. You're going to be putting them inside'; 'the first thing you're going to do when everyone gets back is go over the home work so this would be a marvellous time to get it finished'; 'get out last night's reading assignment'; 'break now, have a snack now'. 'Now we're running overtime. Quick, reading groups. Get your maths papers out'. 'We'll finish now. A new book on Monday'. These interjections are not simply practical features of classroom activity, although they do have specific surface functions in organizing the day where only one teacher takes a class right through. They also, however, help to define what literacy is: they define the organization of texts, papers, and reading and writing materials as the organization of cultural time and space. While they appear to be teaching strategies, they in fact set the boundaries of literacy itself and assert its place within a culturally defined authority structure. The teacher has the authority to bound time and space for the students, and this authority reinforces her control over the definition and bounding of linguistic practices: literacy is placed in relation both to oral discourse and to specific material practices with which it becomes entwined and defined.

In the same voice as she marks phases of time during the day, the teacher sets out procedures for this material practice of literacy: 'When you've finished, put all the papers in the folder I gave you. You're going to be responsible for finding all the things when we're going through it. That's why you have the folder'; 'If you want to write the sentences on lined paper, then take some from your book'. 'Turn over on the back of the paper'. The ending of a session is defined by a combination of linguistic markers and literacy practices: 'Put your scripts in a folder. You may fold it in half once to get it in'.

Oral procedures for finding their way around a written text also combine teacher authority over texts with a 'mix' of oral and written conventions that is not explicitly addressed. It is as though the words were not being spoken but assimilated to the written form:

TEACHER: Top of page 62. What does C's mother do about that? . . . Let's look at page 66 now. I'm sorry, page 64. Read to me the third sentence. That's the third sentence not the third line. How can you find a paragraph? It starts in.

STUDENT: It starts with a capital letter.

TEACHER: Yes, but it also starts in . . . Can you tell me the last word of the sentence? What was that word? Page 59 now. So D. was going home . . . what was the friend's name? . . . the last two lines tell you. Page 60 now. Read what Steve says . . . Bob says that.

Much of this discourse depends upon shared assumptions about the visual perception of a text, its layout and organization – a paragraph 'starts in', page numbers mark the physical boundaries of written material, 'sentences' are visual presences whose opening and closing words can be easily identified (unlike in much oral discourse). The oral representation of the materiality of the written medium becomes a means of organizing actual social relations in the classroom.

Another teacher, getting students to read the parts in a television script, similarly combines oral and written strategies in asserting her authority to determine who has the right to speak at different defined points and where they are in the text:

> TEACHER: Page 5, first column, down near the bottom . . . we'll switch reader when we get to that spot. Narrator for 1, 2 and 3. For 4, 5 and 6 Sarah. M for all those sections David. That should take care of everything up to the end of 6. If you get stuck on a word don't worry about it, everyone can see it and knows it. Try to pronounce it. . . . Wait, remember to read that dark print stuff first, where is it happening now, the dark print tells you that. We'll finish at the end of 7. I'm going to do 7. I know I said we'd finish at 6, but we're going to do to the end of 7.

The visual and linguistic markers for moving around a text dominate the discourse and establish the teacher's authority over the direction readers will take. The text becomes a concrete set of signs on a pathway and students are busy looking for cues to their own involvement and for ending. It is interesting that there is much scope here for the teacher to address metalinguistic features of oral/literate interaction (Fairclough, 1989) and to decode the significance of different print faces and so on but these are not the kinds of metalinguistic issues with which the pedagogic voice is concerned. Rather, it develops procedural skills in moving around texts, asserts who has authority over the text, and reinforces the pressure on students to see written language as something separate and detached.

Homogenization or Variation?

A key question for future research is how the assertion of authority and the allocation of participants to specific roles and relationships are inscribed within particular literacy events and practices. At first, this may lead us to conclude that the conception of literacy associated with schooling and pedagogy, in particular the emphasis on Teaching and Learning, is transforming the rich variety of literacy practices evident in community literacies into a single, homogenized practice. Mothers and children in the home adopt the roles of teachers and learners; a toy is treated not as a source of 'play', to be used according to the cultural conventions associated with leisure, relaxation, childhood, and so on, but instead is located within a framework of teaching and learning, scaffolding the child to future academic achievement; reading a story aloud is transformed by the pedagogic voice from a context of narrative, character, and morality to a prescribed role for the listening child in the achievement of school 'readiness'.

However, as ethnographies of literacy in the community proliferate, a more complex picture may emerge, and we expect to find forms of resistance and alternative literacies alongside 'schooled' literacy. Moreover, it is already apparent that the process of pedagogization of literacy does not derive solely from schools, although its institutional and historical roots are clearly found there, as Cook-Gumperz (1986) and Soltow and Stevens (1981) have demonstrated. It is not simply a matter of how school imposes its version of literacy on the outside world – as we originally imagined and as a rich educational literature has presumed. Rather, the question to be explored is how and why this version of literacy is constructed, assimilated, and internalized in many different contexts, including the school itself. We have tried to suggest ways in which the question of *how* this process is effected may be answered. We conclude with some suggestions as to *why* the process is so important in contemporary American society.

Theoretical considerations: literacy, ideology and nationalism

The new ethnographies of literacy tell us that people can lead full lives without the kinds of literacy assumed in educational and other circles. The reconceptualization of literacy suggested there involves moving away from the dominant view of literacy as having distinctive 'autonomous' characteristics associated intrinsically with schooling and pedagogy. It also entails a shift away from the characterization of the literate person as intrinsically civilized, detached, logical, and so on in contrast with 'illiterates' or those who communicate mainly through oral channels. If the qualities of logic, detachment, abstraction conventionally associated with the acquisition of literacy turn out to be available in oral discourse, as Finnegan (1988) and others have amply demonstrated, or rather in some mix of channels that does not require the conventions and rules usually associated with literacy-in-itself, as we have been suggesting here, then literacy loses some of the status and mystification that currently underpin the investment of vast resources in both teaching and measuring it.

How, then, can we explain the almost obsessive attention to literacy in American society, and why is literacy assumed to be 'functionally necessary' there? One possible answer, suggested by our analysis here of the pedagogization of literacy, is that the language of 'function' disguises and effectively naturalizes the ideological role of literacy in contemporary society. The pedagogized literacy that we have been discussing becomes, then, an organizing concept around which ideas of social identity and value are defined; what kinds of collective identity we subscribe to, what kind of nation we want to belong to, are encapsulated within apparently disinterested accounts of the function, purpose and educational necessity of this kind of literacy. Literacy, in this sense, becomes a symbolic key to many of the society's gravest problems: issues of ethnic identity, conflict, achievement (or underachievement) can be diverted into accounts of how literacy acquisition can be improved and the distribution of literacy enhanced; issues of poverty and unemployment can be turned into questions about why individuals failed to learn literacy at school, or continue to refuse remedial attention as adults, thus diverting blame from institutions to individuals, from power structures to personal morality; issues concerning the effectiveness and achievement of American society as a whole, in comparison with others such as Japan that are seen to be 'overtaking', succeeding where America fails, are located within a framework of educational debate about reading and writing, again diverting attention away from the institutional explanations for budget deficits, space programme failures and productivity declines. All of these issues become focused within a single, overdetermined sign – that of literacy. The signification of literacy has, then, to be decoded not simply in terms of a discourse around education – school quality, teacher performance, testing and evaluation, approaches to writing instruction, and the like – but in terms of discourses of nationalism: it is around the concept of nation and national identity that the social issues currently diverted into the literacy debate essentially focus. To understand the uses and meanings of literacy, then, we need to analyze their relationship to contemporary nationalism.

Indeed, much of the debate about literacy 'standards', currently highlighted in the work of Hirsch (1987, 1988) and Bloome, Puro and Theodorou (1989) in the USA, does make explicit as well as implicit reference to nationalism. Hirsch, for instance, bases his concept of 'cultural literacy' upon the idea of 'a shared national standard'. He likens the hard-won uniformity in economic laws and interstate commerce to the 'literacy uniformity' that is crucial to the formation and underpinning of the nation: 'The two kinds of uniformity are closely allied' (Hirsch, 1988).

Similarly, Ernest Gellner's (1983) account of the growth of the nation-state in the modern world rests upon the privileging of a particular literacy, that purveyed in specific educational institutions:

> Modern industry requires a mobile, literate, technologically equipped population and the modern state is the only agency capable of providing such a work force through its support for a mass, public, compulsory and standardized education system. Modern societies require cultural homogeneity to function. (Quoted in Smith, 1986, p. 10)

Which culture is to provide the model for such homogeneity and which cultures are to be marginalized within this hegemony is not spelled out: it is presented as a question simply of function rather than of power struggles between competing cultures. The question of which literacy is to provide the standard and which literacies are to be marginalized is similarly disguised beneath the discourse of technological need and institutional necessity. And yet, behind their appeal to apparently neutral forces, Gellner and Hirsch make it quite clear that they have in mind a specific culture and a specific literacy – that of their own subculture. The assumed agreement about what constitutes literacy serves to naturalize their own ideological position: it appears not as an argument in favour of their own preferred kind of literacy and culture but as a given fact of modern life, a necessity by which we are all driven. To question their claims would be to undermine the success and achievements of the nation, to challenge its very identity. Within this discourse, an appeal for cultural plurality and literacy variety appears to be a recipe for chaos.

Why this is the case and how these particular views of literacy assert and reproduce their hegemony are the central questions that we hope this chapter has raised, if not resolved. We would like to encourage research into literacy and its relationship with nationalism and with culture that starts not from the premises assumed by

Hirsch, Gellner, and much of the educational literature, but from a more culturally sensitive and politically conscious perspective.

It is, then, within an ideological model of literacy that such research needs to be framed. This model of literacy is situated within the larger ideology of language, of which distinctions between writing, reading and oral events are only sub-categories themselves separated out and defined within the ideology. We do not mean an 'ideology' of language in the weak sense of referring to 'ideas about' language, although these are obviously significant, but in a stronger sense that encompasses the relationship between the individual and the social institution and the mediation of the relationship through sign systems. When we participate in the language of an institution, whether as speakers, listeners, writers, or readers, we become positioned by that language; in that moment of assent, myriad relationships of power, authority, status are implied and reaffirmed. At the heart of this language in contemporary society, there is a relentless commitment to instruction. It is this that frames and constructs what we refer to as the 'pedagogization' of literacy.

Conclusion

We have suggested that research in this area should not focus on the school in isolation but on the conceptualization of literacy in the 'community'. In rethinking concepts of literacy associated with pedagogization, particularly focused around the language of literacy, procedures for its dissemination, and the construction of an autonomous model of literacy, we have come to recognize how they derive not so much from the school itself as from wider cultural and ideological patterns. Within school, the association of literacy acquisition with the child's development of specific social identities and positions; the privileging of written over oral language; the interpretation of 'metalinguistic' awareness in terms of specific literacy practices and grammatical terminology; and the neutralizing and objectification of language that disguises its social and ideological character – all must be understood as essentially *social* processes: they contribute to the construction of a particular kind of citizen, a particular kind of identity, and a particular concept of the nation. The community in its wider sense, including the 'nation' itself, participates in these

ideological constructions through processes that are equally represented as politically neutral, simply educational matters. Parents,
whether helping their children with school tasks or challenging
school control of literacy through local lobbies, reinforce the association of literacy with learning and pedagogy; the construction and
filling of the home space with literacy materials are associated with
specific theories of learning; the kinds of literacy children might be
acquiring from peer groups and the community are marginalized
against the standard of schooled literacy. This reinforcement of
schooled literacy in the community contributes, alongside that of the
school itself, to the construction of identity and personhood in the
modern nation-state. The home and community practices feed back
in turn into school practice, helping to assert and re-fashion there
too the pedagogization of literacy. These, then, are the characteristic
social processes and values through which literacy is construed and
disseminated in mainstream America today, very different processes
and values than those evident from the ethnographies of literacy
currently emerging from research in the Third World, in the history
of America, and in sections of contemporary American society itself.
If we wish to understand the nature and meanings of literacy in our
lives, then, we need more research that focuses on literacy in the
community – in its broadest sense – and on the ideological rather
than the educational implications of the communicative practices in
which it is embedded.

References

Barton, D. and Ivanic. R. (eds) (1991) *Writing in the Community*. Sage:
London.
Barton, D. and Padmore, S. (1991) 'Roles, Networks and Values in Everyday
Writing', in D. Barton and R. Ivanic (eds) *Writing in the Community*.
Sage: London.
Besnier, N. (1989) 'The Encoding of Affect in Nukulaelae Letters', *Text*, vol.
9, no. 1: 69–92.
Bledsoe, C. and Robey, K. (1986) 'Arabic Literacy and Secrecy among the
Mende of Sierra Leone', *Man*, n.s., vol. 21, no. 2: 202–26.
Bloom, A. (1987) *The Closing of the American Mind*. Simon & Schuster:
New York.
Bloome, D. Puro, P. and Theodorou, F. (1989) 'Procedural Display and

Classroom Lessons', *Curriculum Inquiry*, vol. 13, no. 3: 265–91.

Brooks, A.A. (1989, January) 'Too Much, Too Soon: With So Much Emphasis on Structured Learning, Preschoolers are in Danger of Forgetting How To Invent Their Own Games – or Even How To Play, *Parenting*, pp. 74–92.

Bruner, J. (1985) 'Narrative and Paradigmatic Modes of Thought', in E. Eisner (ed.), *Learning and Teaching the Ways of Knowing*. University of Chicago Press: Chicago.

Camitta, M. (1993) 'Vernacular Writing: Varieties of Literacy among Philadelphia High School Students', in B. Street (ed.) *Cross-Cultural Approaches to Literacy*. CUP: Cambridge.

Clanchy, M. (1979) *From Memory to Written Record: England 1066–1307*. Edward Arnold: London.

Collins, J. (1993) 'The Troubled Text: History and Language in American University Basic Writing Programs', in P. Freebody and A. Welch (eds) *Knowledge, Culture and Power: International Perspectives on Literacy as Policy and Practice*. Falmer Press: London.

Cook-Gumperz, J. (1986) *The Social Construction of Literacy*. CUP: Cambridge.

Department of Education and Science (DES) (1988) *English for Ages 5 to 11* (The Cox Report). Her Majesty's Stationery Office: London.

Fairclough, N. (1985) 'Critical and Descriptive Goals in Discourse Analysis', *Journal of Pragmatics*, vol. 9: 739–63.

Fairclough, N. (1989) *Language and Power*. Longman: London.

Fingeret, A. (1983) 'Social Network: a New Perspective on Independence and Illiterate Adults', *Adult Education Quarterly*, vol. 33, no. 3: 133–4.

Finnegan, R. (1988) *Literacy and Orality*. Basil Blackwell: Oxford.

Fishman, J. (1986) 'Nationality–Nationalism and Nation–Nationism', in J. Fishman, C. Ferguson and J. Das Gupta (eds) *Language Problems of Developing Nations*. John Wiley: New York.

Fishman, J. (1991) 'Because This Is Who We Are: Writing in the Arnish Community', in D. Barton and R. Ivanic (eds) *Writing in the Community*. Sage: London.

Gellner, E. (1983) *Nations and Nationalism*. Basil Blackwell: London.

Goody, J. (1986) *The Logic of Writing and the Organization of Society*. CUP: Cambridge.

Graft, H. (1979) *The Literacy Myth: Literacy and Social Structure in the 19th Century City*. Academic Press: London.

Harbsmeier, M. (1989) 'Inventions of Writing', in K. Schousboe and M.T. Larsen (eds) *Literacy and Society*. Akademsig Forlag: Copenhagen.

Heath, S.B. (1983) *Ways with Words*. CUP: Cambridge.

Hill, C. and Parry, K. (1988) 'The Test at the Gate', Occasional Paper. Columbia University: New York.

Hirsch, E.D. (1987) *Cultural Literacy: What Every American Needs to Know*. Houghton Mifflin: Boston.

Hirsch, E.D., Jr. (1988, January) 'Cultural Literacy: Let's Get Specific' [Special issue], *NEA Today*.

Holland, D. and Street B. (1994) 'Assessing Adult Literacy in the UK: 'The Progress Profile', in C. Hill and K. Parry (eds) *From Testing to Assessment: English as an International Language*. Longman: London.

Howard, U. (1991) 'Self, Education and Writing in Nineteenth-Century English Communication', in D. Barton and R. Ivanic (eds) *Writing in the Community*. Sage: London.

Ivanic, R. and Barton, D. (1989) 'The Role of Language Study in Adult Literacy', in J. McCaffery and B. Street (eds) *Literacy Research in the UK*. RaPAL: Lancaster.

King, L. (1994) 'Roots of Identity: Language and Literacy in Mexico,' in B. Street (ed.) *Cross-Cultural Approaches to Literacy*. CUP: Cambridge.

Kulick, D. and Stroud, C. (1993) 'Conceptions and Uses of Literacy in a Papua New Guinea Village', in B. Street (ed.) *Cross-Cultural Approaches to Literacy*. CUP: Cambridge.

Lankshear, C. and Lawler, M. (1987) *Literacy, Schooling and Revolution*. Falmer Press: London.

Lewis, I. (1986) 'Literacy and Cultural Identity in the Horn of Africa: The Somali case', in G. Baumann (ed.) *The Written Word*. Clarendon Press: Oxford.

Maclaren, P. (1986) *Schooling as a Ritual Performance*. RKP: London.

Maybin, J. (1988) 'Peer Group Language in the Classroom', unpublished MA thesis. University of Sussex.

McCaffery, J. and Street, B. (1988) Literacy Research in the UK: Adult and School Perspectives. RaPAL: Lancaster.

Mickulecky, B. (1985) 'The Paston Letters: An Example of Literacy in the 15th Century', unpublished manuscript.

National Academy of Education (1985) *Becoming a Nation of Readers*. NIE: Washington, DC.

Ogbu, J. (1990) 'Cultural Mode, Identity and Literacy', in J.W. Stigler (ed.) *Cultural Psychology*. CUP: Cambridge.

Olson, D., Hildyard, A. and Torrance, N. (1985) *Literacy, Language and Learning*. CUP: Cambridge.

Ong, W. (1982) *Orality and Literacy*. Methuen: London.

Reid, A. (1988) *South East Asia in the Age of Commerce: 1450–1680: Vol. 1. The Lands Below the Winds*. Yale UP: New Haven, Connecticut.

Rockhill, K. (1987) 'Gender, Language and the Politics of Literacy', *British Journal of the Sociology of Language*, vol. 8, no. 2: 153–67.

Rudy, M. (1989) 'The Dynamics of Collaborative Learning of Writing (CLW) in Secondary Classrooms: Control or Cooperation?', unpublished doctoral dissertation, University of Pennsylvania (UMI Dissertation Information Services).

Scribner, S. and Cole, M. (1981) *The Psychology of Literacy*. Harvard UP: Cambridge, Massachusetts

Shuman, A. (1983) *Story-telling Rights*. CUP: Cambridge.

Smith, A. (1986) *The Ethnic Origins of Nations*. Basil Blackwell: Oxford.

Soltow, L. and Stevens, E. (1981) *The Rise of Literacy and the Common School: a Socioeconomic Analysis to 1870*. University of Chicago Press: Chicago.

Street, B. (1985) *Literacy in Theory and Practice*. CUP: Cambridge.

Street, B. (1988) 'Literacy Practices and Literacy Myths', in R. Saljo (ed.) *The Written World*. Springer Press: Berlin/New York.

Street, B. (ed.) (1993) *Cross-Cultural Approaches to Literacy*. CUP: Cambridge.

Street, B. and Besnier, N. (1994) 'Aspects of Literacy', in T. Ingold (ed.) *Companion Encyclopedia of Anthropology*. Routledge: London.

Tannen, D. (1982) *Spoken and Written Language: Exploring Orality and Literacy*. Ablex: Norwood, New Jersey.

Tannen, D. (1985) 'Relative Focus on Involvement in Oral and Written Discourse', in D. Olson et al. (eds) *Literacy, Language and Learning*. CUP: Cambridge.

Teale, W. and Sulzby, E. (1987) 'Literacy Acquisition in Early Childhood: the Roles of Access and Mediation in Storybook Reading', in D. Wagner (ed.) *The Future of Literacy in a Changing World*. Pergamon: Oxford.

Varenne, H. and McDermott, R. (1983), 'Why Sheila Can Read: Structure and Indeterminacy in the Structure of Familial Literacy.' in B. Schieffelin and P. Gilmore (eds) *Ethnographic Perspective in the Acquisition of Literacy*. Ablex: Norwood.

Weinstein-Shr, G. (1993) 'Literacy and Social Process: a Community in Transition', in B. Street (ed.) *Cross-Cultural Approaches to Literacy*. CUP: Cambridge.

Wells, G. (1985) 'Preschool Literacy-related Activities and Success in School', in D. Olson et al. (eds) *Literacy, Language and Learning*. CUP: Cambridge.

Wertsch, J.V. (ed.) (1981) *The Concept of Activity in Soviet Psychology*. Sharpe: White Plains, New York.

Yin-Yee Ko, D. (1989) 'Toward a Social History of Women in Seventeenth-Century China', unpublished doctoral dissertation, Stanford University.

6 The Implications of the New Literacy Studies for Pedagogy

I would like to relate some of the developments in what has come to be called the 'New Literacy Studies' in recent years to some of the debates currently taking place regarding the role of literacy and education. I am frequently asked to relate directly the theoretical principles I am outlining to practise in teaching literacy and this chapter makes some attempt to respond. I am conscious of the limitations of my own experience in addressing such a question. I have, however, been involved in practice – particularly in adult literacy in the UK and recently in developing countries, while the responses to my representations of literacy have themselves led to some acquaintance with the educational agendas that this piece addresses. A major thrust of this book has also been that traditional divisions between academic research and practitioner research need to be broken down, and I see this chapter as congruent with that approach. I will begin, then, with a brief outline of the conceptual apparatus that is becoming familiar in the New Literacy Studies, and deal briefly with some of the problems it has raised. Then I will consider the implications of viewing literacy in this way for some current issues in education, including the significance of different educational philosophies – whole language, Freirean, etc. – and the question of access to dominant literacy.

I will outline here the aspects of my arguments about the autonomous and ideological models of literacy that are relevant to educational practice and policy and then detail some recent developments in the concepts that I find helpful in applying them in this context. As I have argued above, a great deal of the thinking about literacy in a previous generation has assumed that literacy with a big 'L' and a single 'y' was a single autonomous thing that had consequences for personal and social development. The autonomous model of literacy has been a dominant feature of educational and development theory. One of the reasons for referring to this position as an autonomous model of literacy is that it represents itself as though it is not a position located ideologically at all, as though it is just natural. One of the reasons why I want to call the counter-position ideological is precisely in order to signal that we are not simply talking here about technical features of the written process or the oral process. What we are talking about are competing models and assumptions about reading and writing processes, which are always embedded in power relations. The agenda, then, is contested already. There is variation in literacy across a whole range of different practices, contexts, domains and in each case there are 'competing discourses' (Lee, 1992). Two working concepts that have enabled researchers to apply this general principle to specific data have been the concepts of literacy events and literacy practices. The concept of *literacy events* described above (p. 2) has stressed the importance of a mix of oral and literate features in everyday communication. Lectures, for instance, represent a classic literacy event: the lecturer reads from notes, perhaps; an overhead slide projects different types of notes; occasionally people might look up at the overhead, and look down and write a note; read their notes and listen again to the speaker; some might file their notes away somewhere in a bureaucracy; some might throw them in the waste-paper basket. The whole is, in a sense, greater than the sum of its parts and is underpinned by systems of ideas and organization that are not necessarily made explicit in the immediate discourse. This is where I have felt it important to draw attention to the ideological aspect: these are any kinds of conventions which people internalize – we all know how tightly controlled the conventions are in everyday literacy events such as encounters with bureaucracy, or in seminars or meetings. They become more apparent at times of political resistance – feminist and other movements, for instance, in resisting dominant speech/ writing conventions, work to make them explicit as a step towards changing them.

Thus we have culturally constructed models of the literacy event in our minds. I want to use the concept of *literacy practices* to indicate this level of the cultural uses and meanings of reading and writing. Literacy practices I would take as referring not only to the event itself but the conceptions of the reading and writing process that people hold when they are engaged in the event. The distinction between literacy practices and literacy events has been well summarized and further elaborated in *Writing in the Community* (Barton and Ivanic, 1991). So, armed with those two concepts, literacy events and literacy practices, within the framework of an ideological model, it seems to me possible to start doing comparative research as well as to organize programmes and develop curricula in a more socially conscious and explicit way.

What I want to avoid, in looking at the cultural aspect of literacy, is recreating the reified list – here's a culture, here's its literacy; here's another culture, here's its literacy (cf. Thornton, 1988). That is one of the problems that have arisen with the notion of multiple literacies. The notion of multiple literacies is crucial in challenging the autonomous model. We have to be able to indicate that the notion of a single literacy with a big 'L' and a single 'y' is only one subculture's view and there are varieties of literacy practices. But once you slip into the notion of multiple literacies you then begin to move towards culture as a listed inventory. I indicate just a few of the different ways in which the notion of multiple literacies has been defined recently to indicate the conceptual as well as ideological difficulties entailed.

The work by Kirsch and Jungeblut in America (1986), *Profiles of America's Young Adults*, talks of three literacies: reading, writing and numeracy, with possibly a fourth, document processing. In Australia frameworks and competency scales for assessing literacy levels are presently being researched (Griffin, 1990). Griffin, for instance, claims explicitly that there are four literacies: literacy for knowledge, literacy for self-expression, literacy for practical purposes, literacy for public debate. Heath (1983a), working in the Piedmont Carolinas, talked about three communities, each having a literacy. In a sense, the work I was doing in Iran (see above, chapter 3), talking about three different literacies – *maktab* literacy, school literacy, commercial literacy – could take on that same characteristic if we assume that each literacy is associated with a different community. A similar view is to be found among some researchers in the New Literacy Studies in America. Miriam Camitta (1993) for instance, researching adolescent literacies in and out of school, talks about vernacular literacy and schooled literacy, where the vernacular literacy represents a resistance to the dominant mode by adolescents who develop their own literacy practices separately. Barton and Ivanic (1991), in the book *Writing in the Community*, talk about 'domains' of literacy. Community literacy has become quite a key concept in the Lancaster research programme. Harvey Graff, a keen student of the proliferating metaphors of literacy, recently came across the phrase 'emotional literacy', while a recent radio broadcast on the death of a famous film producer referred to him as 'film literate'. The further these usages get away from the social practices of reading and writing, the more evident it is that the term 'literacy' is being used in a narrow, moral and functional sense to mean cultural competence or skills. While this may be a telling example of the ideological ways in which the term is used in given social contexts, it is not much help at an analytical level when we are trying to compare one set of literacy practices with another: it becomes easy to collude with the imposition of specific cultural meanings on to the literacy practices of other people for whom these meanings are quite inappropriate. The extensions and metaphors serve to disguise the ideological underpinnings of our own meanings and uses of literacy.

To avoid the pitfalls in these extensions of the notion of multiple literacies, I have tried to develop the notion of dominant literacies, in opposition to 'marginalized' literacies, on the analogy with some of the work in sociolinguistics around the notion of dominant language (Grillo, 1989). If you talk about 'standard', it looks as though that is naturally the one that we should all be acquiring. If you talk about dominant language, you're asking the questions, how did it become dominant? how does it reproduce itself? how does it contest with other, marginalized languages? A great deal of current research in ethnography of literacy practices is beginning to explore the associations between cultural conventions, literacy practices, notions of self, person and identity and struggles over power. We need, then, not just 'cultural' models of literacy but 'ideological' ones, in the sense that in all of these cases, the uses and meanings of literacy entail struggles over particular identities up against other identities, often imposed ones.

Implications for pedagogy and educational policy

All of this has huge implications for pedagogy, and I will suggest some of the ways in which this might be explored. This account is based on the argument developed elsewhere (Gee, Luke, Freebody and Street, forthcoming), concerned not so much with providing a fixed, proper way to view literacy, but a heuristic framework within which teachers, practitioners, teacher educators and programme planners can theorize their practice in the contexts of the specific cultural differences, localities and politics they are faced with. Many of the arguments with regard to formal schooling have been dealt with by Luke and others (Luke, 1988; de Castell, Luke, A. and Luke, C., 1989), in showing that the history of 'schooled literacy' (cf. Cook-Gumperz, 1986) has a specific ideological history, related to the gendered construction of appropriate selves for particular political cultures. A reframing of literacy as a critical social practice requires us to take account of these historical as well as cross-cultural perspectives in classroom practice and to help students to locate their literacy practices, somewhat in the way that the Critical Language Awareness (Fairclough, 1992) approach helps locate language practices more generally.

It seems to follow from all of this that the teacher, the curriculum designer and the programme developer, whether in industrialized societies facing 'new times' or in 'development' programmes, need to have an understanding not only of educational theory, but of linguistic theory, of literacy theory and of social theory. In these contexts there inevitably will be implicit assumptions about cultural relations, identity etc., but to maintain any kind of control of what we are doing, we need to make them explicit: and to work through their implications for pedagogy, school literacy and for the social relations teachers have with their students. I will briefly touch on a number of different approaches to teaching literacy in the light of these perspectives: schooled literacy, the Freireian approach, the language experience approach, and the genre approach. Much of what I am saying about literacy practices also applies to numeracy practices, although there is not space here to explore this (cf. Baker and Street, 1993).

With regard to schooled literacy, it is clear that in general the autonomous model of literacy has dominated curriculum and pedagogy. As Freebody and others have shown (Freebody, 1992), apparently innocent texts for infants, questions by teachers and the emphasis on 'correct' spelling and on linguistic detail, are ways of maintaining discipline. Learning precise phonemic distinctions is not just a technical prerequisite of reading and writing but a key way of training new members of the polity *how* to learn and how to discern other distinctions, to make appropriate cultural discriminations in

societies that are increasingly heterogeneous. These secondary discourses, as Gee calls the literacies delivered by state institutions,
enable a centralizing state to assert homogeneity against the heteroge-
neity evident in the variety of primary discourses into which communities socialize their members (Gee, 1990). Teaching awareness of these
conflicts and of the ways in which literacy practices are sites of
ideological contest, is itself already a challenge to the dominant
autonomous model that disguises such processes.

Paulo Freire's approach to learning in Third World literacy campaigns has attempted to challenge this model. Criticizing the 'bank-
ing' approach to learning, that assumed knowledge was a fixed set of
facts to be deposited in the learner, he has advocated an approach
that starts from consciousness-raising, enabling the poor and oppressed to explore and analyze the sources of their oppression.
Literacy classes would begin with discussion of key concepts in the
local context, such as 'favela' (slum) in shanty towns. The animator
would discuss with class members what such concepts mean in their
context, how it is that they come to live in such conditions, where
the responsibility lies for the gross poverty experienced by so many.
Once the words themselves had become familiar in this critical sense,
the animator would then begin to write them down for the students.
In Portuguese, the language in which Freire began his work, and also
in Spanish, in which it has been particularly influential, words are
built up out of syllables so that a word such as 'favela' can be broken
down into parts and then each part – fav-el-a – rebuilt with other
syllables – fav + el + o – to make new words. Students can quickly
learn to copy the letters of such key words and then make their own
new words, moving on to sentence building. This approach, a
combination of general political socialization with specific language
techniques, has been highly influential in a number of literacy campaigns in the past twenty years and is also being employed in many
adult literacy classes in industrialized societies (Barton and Hamilton,
1990). From the perspective I am developing here, however, there are
a number of problems that need to be addressed. Prinsloo, a South
African educator, points out some of the problems with using this
syllabic approach almost exclusively: lessons on word building tend
to go on indefinitely without learners developing reading and writing
habits that are embedded in real-use contexts. The move to reading
and writing seriously for meaning gets delayed for so long that
learners sometimes despair. He concludes that there is an 'urgent

need for development of method to include aspects of language experience approach to literacy teaching together with the phonetical drills of the Freireian approach' (Prinsloo, 1990, p. 14).

Similar criticisms can be found from other parts of the world. Bourgois (1986), writing of the Nicaraguan Literacy Crusade which was one of the more spectacular successes of a modified Freireian approach, points out, as an anthropologist, how culturally specific the chosen key words can be and how difficult it is for programme organizers and teachers really to know what the key words in a culture are and what they mean. The Sandinistas organized their campaign after the revolution (cf. Lankshear and Lawler, 1987) in the midst of revolutionary fervour that many commentators have argued is the key ingredient for success of the 'mass' campaign (cf. Bhola, 1984). But they failed at first to recognize that those who lived on the Atlantic Coast belonged to quite different cultural and language groupings than the dominant Spanish-speaking peoples who had been involved in the revolution. For them the key phrase 'Sandino is the Hero of the Revolution' was as meaningless and as much part of Managuan hegemony as had been the grosser propoganda of the previous Samosa regime (Freeland, 1990). The Freireian approach is vulnerable to such culturally blind manipulation by activists imbued with ideological fervour and believing so strongly that they are 'empowering' 'ignorant' peasants that they fail to see their own cultural and political domination. Rogers, reviewing a recent book on literacy and power in South American literacy campaigns (Archer and Costello, 1990), makes a similar point. Against the apparent belief of the authors and of many of the practitioners whose work they describe, that literacy is inevitably empowering, Rogers argues:

> Until we know the nature of the power used by the oppressor, we cannot know whether literacy can or cannot do anything to relieve that oppression. By a close study of the nature and causes of poverty, it seems to be increasingly accepted that literacy can do little to relieve the first stages of extreme poverty (though it contributes mightily to the second and higher levels of increasing prosperity). Similarly, what we need now is to study power first, not literacy. If literacy in itself does possess the power to empower, as is so often claimed, then more is needed than the case studies in this book to demonstrate it. But I am beginning to doubt it; for the elites who hold power do not do so on

the basis of literacy. They often use literacy to buttress their power; but they have many other weapons. If one hundred percent literacy was achieved in a country like Cuba, for example, would democracy be advanced one bit? I doubt it. (Rogers, 1990, p. 34)

A similar argument might be used to qualify some of the faith in teaching children the dominant literacies or the 'genres of power' put forward by some advocates of the genre approach to schooling and literacy in Australia. Some there would argue that children cannot learn to question the power structures of the society they inhabit until *after* they have learned these genres. The teacher's task, then, is to impart knowledge of the traditional forms of reading and writing – the dominant literary forms, the genres of expository prose and essay-text writing, the ways of composing letters to business organizations – in order to empower their students. Only then can those students be in a position to question whether these forms are biased against their particular backgrounds – in gender or ethnic terms for instance – and work to change them. There are a number of problems with this 'wait for critique' approach. Gee (1990) points out that much of the linguistic triviality that goes to make up such genres and to mark social groups as separate (phonology, spelling, surface grammar etc.) is learnt in 'socially situated practices' (p. 149) not in the classroom: hence 'they cannot be "picked up" later, outside the full context of an early apprenticeship (at home, not at school)'. This is the problem with J.D. Hirsch's much-publicized notion of 'cultural literacy', which is strikingly similar to that proposed by those on the other end of the political spectrum as the 'genres of power': 'he is right', says Gee, 'that without having mastered an extensive list of trivialities people can be (and often are) excluded from "goods" controlled by dominant groups in the society; he is wrong that this can be taught (in a classroom of all places!) apart from the socially situated practices that these groups have incorporated into their homes and daily lives' (Gee, 1990, p. 149). A further problem with the 'wait for critique' approach is highlighted by Rogers' arguments above: even when children have acquired the powerful genres, there is no guarantee that they will become empowered: the goal-posts may shift, as many women and those from ethnic minorities and working-class backgrounds have discovered in the USA and UK, where statistics show that women and people of colour who have university degrees cannot obtain the kinds of jobs achieved by white men with comparable qualifications. In Gee's terms, if the markers of separation are indeed often trivial, then it is not very difficult for those in power to change them as new cohorts of 'outsiders' learn the spelling, grammar and phonology of the dominant groups.

A further problem with the dominant literacy position that is highlighted by the approach being put forward here, is the fact that assumptions are being made about the nature and uses of reading and writing without actual ethnographic knowledge. There are a number of powerful genres, not just a single autonomous literacy and we know very little about how they operate – in the Stock Exchange for instance, or in higher reaches of commerce and government. One might speculate that these in-house, abbreviated literacies through which those already confident of power communicate, are not the same as those laborious and explicit genres being taught in schools. After all, as many pupils know, the teachers who impart these genres have evidently themselves failed to achieve positions of power in their society. There is much research to be done yet on the actual relations between specific genres and the holding of power, financial and political. To lead students to believe that there is a one-way relationship between particular genres taught in school and those positions is to set them up for disappointment and disillusion.

There is a further argument, brought out in the work of Luke and Freebody and central to the ideological model of literacy, that learning literacy is not just about acquiring content but about learning a process. Every literacy is learnt in a specific context in a particular way and the modes of learning, the social relationships of student to teacher are modes of socialization and acculturation. The student is learning cultural models of identity and personhood, not just how to decode script or to write a particular hand. If that is the case, then leaving the critical process until after they have learnt many of the genres of literacy used in that society is putting off, possibly for ever, the socialization into critical perspective. When exactly will most students revise and criticize their school learning if not during the process of experiencing it? Griffin (1990), in describing stages or levels of literacy for purposes of developing assessment instruments, argues that 'empowerment may not occur until individuals proceed past the access and required levels to a level where they are able to set the parameters on what literacy skills are required' (p. 22). This approach, in which liberal technicists line up with radical genre theorists, is, I believe, fundamentally flawed and deeply conservative. There are problems with the concepts of 'stages' and 'levels' that are coming to dominate discourses on literacy, and with the theories of power, of literacy and of socialization that underpin these approaches. This is well articulated by Sue Newman:

> Because stage-level models are generally based on middle class or mainstream definitions of standard or normative behaviour, they also ignore the political aspects of literacy development by failure to acknowledge that people are often denied comparable access to a particular literacy because of race, class or gender. Benefits of higher levels of literacy are cited without acknowledging that such benefits may not be identical for those who attain them, again because of differential status within a society. (Newman, 1992, p. 13)

An approach that sees literacy as critical social practice would make explicit from the outset both the assumptions and the power relations on which these models of literacy are based. In contrast to the argument that learners are not 'ready' for such critical interpretation until they reach higher stages or levels, I would argue that teachers have a social obligation to do so. This is only possible on the assumption that skilled teachers can facilitate critical perspectives in appropriate language and communicative forms as readily as traditionalists can impart genres, levels, contents and skills within a conservative view of literacy. The introduction of Critical Language Awareness and of Literacy as Critical Social Practice can, I believe, facilitate this process. Introducing this into the classroom is not a luxury but a necessity.

References

Archer, D. and Costello, P. (1990) *Literacy and Power*. Earthscan: London.

Baker, D. and Street, B. (1993) 'Literacy and Numeracy', in *Encyclopedia of Education*. Pergamon Press: Oxford.

Barton, D. and Hamilton, M. (1990) *Researching Literacy in Industrialised Countries: Trends and Prospects*. UNESCO, IBE: Hamburg.

Barton, D. and Ivanic, R. (eds) (1991) *Writing in the Community*. Sage: London.

Bell, J. (ed.) (1990) *TESL Talk: ESL Literacy*, vol. 20, no. 1. Ontario, Canada.

Benhabib, S. (1992) *Situating the Self: Gender, Community and Postmodernism in Contemporary Theory*. Polity Press: London.

Besnier, N. (1989) 'Literacy and Feelings: the Encoding of Affect in Nukulaelae Letters', *Text*, vol. 9, no. 1: 69–92.

Besnier, N. (1990) 'Literacy and the Notion of Person on Nukulaelae Atoll', *American Anthropologist*, no. 93.

Bhola, H.S. (1984) *Campaigning for Literacy*. UNESCO: Paris.

Bloome, D. (ed.) (1989) *Classrooms and Literacy*. Ablex: Norwood, New Jersey.

Boonzaier, E. and Sharp, J. (eds) (1988) *South African Keywords*. David Philip: Cape Town.

Bourgois, P. (1986) 'The Miskitu of Nicaragua: Politicized Ethnicity', *Anthropology Today*, vol. 2, no. 2.

Camitta, M. (1993) 'Vernacular Writing: Varieties of Literacy among Philadelphia High School Students', in B. Street (ed.) *Cross-Cultural Approaches to Literacy*. CUP: Cambridge.

Carrithers, M. (ed.) (1985) *The Category of the Person*. CUP: Cambridge.

Cascardi, A. (1992) *The Subject of Modernity*. CUP: Cambridge.

de Castell, S., Luke, A. and Luke, C. (eds) (1989) *Language, Authority and Criticism: Readings on the School Textbook*. Falmer Press: Brighton.

Chick, K. (ed.) (1990) *Searching for Relevance: Contextual Issues in Applied Linguistics in Southern Africa*. SAALA: Natal.

Cook-Gumperz, J. (ed.) (1986) *The Social Construction of Literacy*. CUP: Cambridge.

Czerniewska, P. (1992) *Learning About Writing*. Blackwell: Oxford.

Dombey, H. and Robinson, M. (eds) (1992) *Literacy for the 21st Century*. Literacy Centre, Brighton Polytechnic: Brighton.

Eagleton, T. (1990) *Ideology: an Introduction*. Verso: London.

Elliott, A. (1992) 'Finding One's Self in a Self-Less World', *The Times Higher Education Supplement*, 10 July 1992.

Fairclough, N. (ed.) (1992) *Critical Language Awareness*. Longman: London.

Finnegan, R. (1973) 'Literacy Versus Non-literacy: the Great Divide', in R. Finnegan and B. Horton (eds) *Modes of Though*. OUP: London.

Finnegan, R. (1988) *Literacy and Orality*. Blackwell: Oxford.

la Fontaine, J. (1985) 'Person and Individual: Some Anthropological Reflections', in M. Carrithers (ed.) *The Category of the Person*. CUP: Cambridge.

Freebody, P. (1992) 'Assembling the Competent Reader: The Critical Teacher', in *The Right to Literacy*, vol. 1 of Conference Papers from the Australian Council for Adult Literacy Conference, Sydney. New South Wales Adult Literacy and Numeracy Council Inc.: Sydney.

Freebody, P. and Welch, A. (1993) *Knowledge, Culture and Power: Inter-*

national Perspectives on Literacy as Policy and Practice. Falmer Press: London.

Freeland, J. (1990) *The Atlantaic Coast in the Nicaraguan Revolution*. WUS: London.

Gee, J. (1990) *Social Linguistics and Literacies: Ideology in Discourses*. Falmer Press: Brighton.

Gee, J., Luke, A., Freebody, P. Street, B. (forthcoming) *Literacy as Critical Social Practice*. Falmer Press: London.

Geertz, C. (1984) 'From the Native's Point of View: On the Nature of Anthropological Understanding', in *Local Knowledge*. Basic Books: New York.

Graff, H. (1987) *The Legacies of Literacy: Continuities and Contradictions in Western Culture and Society*. Indiana UP: Bloomington, Indiana.

Griffin, P. (1990) *Adult Literacy and Numeracy Competency Scales*. Assessment Research Centre, Phillip Institute of Technology: Victoria, Australia.

Grillo, R. (1989) *Dominant Languages*. CUP: Cambridge.

Hamilton, M. and Barton, D. (1985) 'Social and Cognitive Factors in the Development of Writing', in A. Lock and C. Peters (eds) *The Handbook of Human Symbolic Evolution*. OUP: Oxford.

Heath, S.B. (1982a) 'What No Bedtime Story Means: Narrative Skills at Home and at School', *Language in Society*, vol. 11.

Heath, S.B. (1982b) 'Protean Shapes in Literacy Events', in D. Tannen (ed.) *Spoken and Written Language: Exploring Orality and Literacy*. Ablex: Norwood, New Jersey.

Heath, S.B. (1983a) *Ways with Words*. CUP: Cambridge.

Heath, S.B. (1983b) 'The Achievement of Pre-School Literacy for Mother and Child', in H. Goelman, A. Oberg and F. Smith (eds) *Awakening to Literacy*. Heinemann: New York.

Hill, C. and Parry, K. (1988) 'Ideological and "Pragmatic" Models of Assessment', Columbia University, Teachers' College, *Occasional Papers*, no. 1 and in *Linguistics in Education*, vol. 1, no. 3, 1989.

Hill, C. and Parry, K. (in press) *From Testing to Assessment: English as an International Language*. Longman: London.

Hirsch, E.D. Jr. (1987) *Cultural Literacy: What Every American Needs to Know*. Houghton Mifflin: Boston.

Horsman, J. (1989) 'From the Learner's Voice: Women's Experience of Il/ Literacy', in M. Taylor and J. Draper (eds) *Adult Literacy Perspectives*. Culture Concepts Inc.: Ontario.

Hutton, B. (ed.) (1992) *Adult Basic Education in South Africa*. OUP: Cape Town.

Kimberley, K., Meek, M. and Miller, J. (1992) *New Readings: Contributions to an Understanding of Literacy*. A&C Black: London.

Kirkpatrick, J. (1983) *The Marquesan Notion of the Person*. UMI Research Press: Ann Arbor, Michigan.

Kirsch, I. and Jungeblut, A. (1986) *Profiles of America's Young Adults.* NAEP: Princeton, New Jersey.

Kulick, D. and Stroud, C. (1990) 'Conceptions and Uses of Literacy in a Papua New Guinean Village', in B. Street (ed.) *Cross-Cultural Approaches to Literacy.* CUP: Cambridge.

Lankshear, C. and Lawler, M. (1987) *Literacy, Schooling and Revolution.* Falmer Press: London.

Lash, S. and Friedman, J. (1992) *Modernity and Identity.* Blackwell: Oxford.

Lee, D. (1992) *Competing Discourses: Perspective and Ideology in Language.* Longman: London.

Luke, A. (1988) *Literacy, Textbooks and Ideology.* Falmer Press: Brighton.

McCaffery, J. and Street, B. (1988) *Literacy Research in the UK: Adult and School Perspectives.* RaPAL: Lancaster.

Mace, J. (1979) *Talking About Literacy.* Routledge: London.

Meek, M. (1991) *On Being Literate.* Bodley Head: London.

Miller, C., Raynham, S.A. and Schaffes A. (1991) *Breaking the Frame: Readings in South African Education in the Eighties.* OUP: Cape Town.

Newman, S. (1992) 'Bringing the Book to Life: Southern Women's Literacies', PhD dissertation, University of Pennsylvania.

Ong, W. (1982) *Literacy and Orality: the Technologizing of the Word.* Methuen: New York/London.

Prinsloo, M. (1990) 'ABE in S. Africa', unpublished manuscript.

Rockhill, K. (1987a) 'Gender, Language and the Politics of Literacy', *British Journal of the Sociology of Education*, vol. 8, no. 2.

Rockhill, K. (1987b) 'Literacy as Threat/Desire: Longing to be SOMEBODY', in J.S. Gaskell and A. McLaren (eds) *Women and Education: a Canadian Perspective.* Detselig: Calgary.

Rogers, A. (1990) 'Review of *Literacy and Power*', *British Association for Literacy in Development Bulletin*, vol. 5, no. 1: 23–35.

Rogers, A. (1992) *Adults Learning for Development.* Cassell: London.

Rutherford, J. (ed.) (1990) *Identity: Community, Culture, Difference.* Lawrence & Wishart: London.

Scribner, S. and Cole, M. (1981) *The Psychology of Literacy.* Harvard UP: Boston.

Shuman, A. (1983) 'Collaborative Literacy in an Urban, Multi-ethnic Neighbourhood', in D. Wagner (ed.) *Literacy and Ethnicity, International Journal for the Sociology of Language*, vol. 42. Mouton: New York.

Shuman, A. (1986) *Storytelling Rights: the Uses of Oral and Written Texts by Urban Adolescents.* CUP: Cambridge.

Street, B. (1984) *Literacy in Theory and Practice.* CUP: Cambridge.

Street, B. (1987) 'Literacy and Social Change: the Significance of Social Context in the Development of Literacy Programmes', in D. Wagner (ed.) *The Future of Literacy.* Pergamon Press: Oxford.

Street, B. (1998a) 'A Critical Look at Walter Ong and the "Great Divide"', *Literacy Research Center Newsletter*, vol. 4, no. 1. University of Pennsylvania.

Street, B. (1988b) 'Literacy Practices and Literacy Myths', in R. Saljo (ed.) *The Written World: Studies in Literate Thought and Action*. Springer-Verlag: Berlin/New York.

Street, B. (1993) (ed.) *Cross-Cultural Approaches to Literacy*. CUP: Cambridge.

Street, B. and J. (1991) 'The Schooling of Literacy', in D. Barton and R. Ivanic (eds) *Writing in the Community*. Sage: London.

Tannen, D. (1985) 'Relative Focus on Involvement in Oral and Written Discourse', in D. Olson and N. Torrance (eds) *Literacy, Language and Learning*. CUP: Cambridge.

Thornton, R. (1988) 'Culture: a Contemporary Definition', in E. Boonzaier and J. Sharp (eds) *South African Keywords*. David Philip: Cape Town.

Wagner, D. (ed.) (1983) *Literacy and Ethnicity, International Journal of the Sociology of Language*, vol. 42. Mouton: New York.

Weinstein-Shr, G. (1992) 'Literacy and Social Process: a Community in Transition', in B. Street (ed.) *Cross-Cultural Approaches to Literacy*. CUP: Cambridge.

Wertsch, J. (ed.) (1991) *Voices of the Mind*. Harvester, Wheatsheaf: London.

Willinsky, J. (1990) *The New Literacy*. Routledge: London.

Section 4:

Towards a Critical Framework

Introduction

The final Section brings together the assumptions and concepts employed in the earlier sections and proposes a critical framework for further study. It critically examines some key theoretical positions that, I argue, have dominated literacy studies for too long. Against these I argue for an 'ideological' model of literacy that is methodologically and theoretically sensitive to local variation in literacy practices and that is able to comprehend people's own uses and meanings of reading and writing. The message of this last section of the book, then, is that in order to understand the nature and role of literacy practices in real social contexts, we need to challenge the theories on which much assumed 'common sense' about literacy has rested and to make explicit the premises on which an alternative account can be developed. The chapters above, while attempting to free us from some of the restrictive traditions and conventions traditionally associated with literacy studies, represent mainly an attempt to build on the positive work in the field of linguistics, anthropology and education cited there in order to suggest new directions for literacy research and practice.

Chapter 7: A Critical Look at Walter Ong and the 'Great Divide'

This chapter attempts a further elaboration of the theoretical debates over a 'great divide' through critical analysis of the work of a key author in the field – Walter J. Ong. Ong has been extremely influential in literacy studies, reinforcing the 'great divide' between orality and literacy and making grand claims for the social and cognitive consequences of literacy. In the USA in particular, his analysis provides the theoretical underpinnings for a great deal of work in both theoretical and practical spheres. The article summarizes Ong's arguments and then analyzes them at three levels: methodological, empirical and theoretical. At a methodological level, it is argued that Ong employs something of the 'if I were a horse' thinking that characterized nineteenth-century travellers' tales and anthropology: the basic problem here is that if the observer has no first-hand experience of the people whose thinking he is trying to replicate imaginatively, then in effect the account becomes a reflection of the writer's own culture and own thinking. With regard to accounts of supposedly 'purely oral' culture, Ong's argument also encounters the fundamental contradiction that he himself is writing from within a literate culture. The social evolutionary character of the accounts is also examined critically. At an empirical level, Ong's account of 'literate society' turns out on examination to be an account of the particular literate practices of a subculture within his own society, specifically the academic subculture of which he himself is a part. Furthermore, the accounts we have of other societies, with different 'mixes' of oral/literate practices, suggests that they do not lack the logic, detachment, self-consciousness, abstraction and the other fundamental cognitive and social abilities that Ong attributes to (academic) literacy. At a theoretical level, as we have seen, recent scholarship has suggested that it is more precise to think of oral/ literate interactions, rather than to search for pure examples of either orality or literacy on their own. Ong, nevertheless, argues that literacy in itself is unique and different in kind from orality, in that it 'fixes' the evanescent nature of sound and experience. I argue in contrast that literacy is not unique in this regard: language in general and various forms of picturing, rituals, stories etc., share this characteristic. Arguments about the particular character of alphabetic writing systems are also examined and it is argued that all writing systems have conventions that approximate to precision while retaining much ambiguity: there appears to be a continuum in the ways in which coding systems represent the various features of sound systems, rather than a great divide as Ong argues. It is difficult to envisage how one system might have greater consequences for fundamental cognitive processes than another.

The reason for dwelling on Ong's arguments in such detail is that they often underlie less self-conscious accounts of literacy in the fields of education and development and in the ethnographic and empirical descriptions of literacy practices. The examination of literacy practices in earlier chapters derived, to some extent, from the critical encounter with theoretical arguments such as those of Ong and Goody. The positive message that I hope emerges from this book builds upon that critical encounter.

Chapter 8: Literacy Practices and Literacy Myths

The final chapter takes note of some recent works on literacy that have moved towards the greater awareness of 'context' advocated here. However, it warns that in some cases the shift may be more rhetorical than real: in a number of those works 'context' is often treated as either a narrow account of specific interactions or networks, or as an 'add on', once the basic features of literacy have been described. In challenging this failure to come to grips with the full meaning of 'context' and its significance for literacy studies, despite some notable advances and developments from earlier perspectives, the chapter clarifies the concepts of 'autonomous' and 'ideological' models. It is argued that these models do not set up a dichotomy in the field, rather that all models of literacy can be understood within an ideological framework and that those termed 'autonomous' only appear on the surface to be neutral and value free. In this sense, it is those who want to retain an 'autonomous' view of literacy who are responsible for a dichotomy: those who subscribe to the ideological model do not deny the significance of technical aspects of reading and writing, such as decoding, sound/shape correspondence and reading 'difficulties', rather they argue that these features of literacy are always embedded in particular social practices: the socialization process through which reading and writing are acquired and the power relations between groups engaged in differing literacy practices are central to the understanding of specific issues and 'problems'.

The chapter also returns to the question raised by many literacy scholars and summarized in the Introduction of the book, concerning the difference between oral and literate modes. Again it is argued that these differences have been overstated; that very often characteristics attributed to one mode rather than the other are in fact features of the social context in which they are employed and that in other contexts those features might be attributed to another mode. Examples of cohesion in oral discourse and of supposedly 'oral-like' features in written discourse are discussed with particular reference to the work of Deborah Tannen. In conclusion it is claimed that the notion of a 'great divide' still persists within many accounts in the field, even though it has often been rejected at the overt level and despite the fact that in its most extreme forms – as evident in the work of Goody, Ong etc. – the problems it raises are apparent. Recent developments in methodology, in ethnography and in discourse analysis, combined with recent developments in theory in anthropology and in sociolinguistics, may provide a framework from which to research literacy practices in a depth and detail that will allow for future generalizations that avoid the problems of the 'great divide' and of the 'autonomous' model. The arguments and the examples described in this book are intended to help us move in that direction.

7 A Critical Look at Walter Ong and the 'Great Divide'

The work of Walter Ong, particularly his version of the 'great divide' between orality and literacy, has dominated the approach to literacy, not only in academic circles, but also in more powerful domains, such as the 'reading' lobby, development agencies, and those responsible for schooling and 'illiteracy' programmes, particularly in the USA. It is important to confront Ong's views directly, to test their validity against current research and theory, and to ask why they are still so powerful. This chapter is intended to provide a few initial suggestions as to what such a project might involve.

Ong's views have been expressed over a number of years in a variety of books and articles, but the most accessible and 'popular' version has been his *Orality and Literacy: The Technologizing of the Word* (1982), and I will use this as a reference point, partly because it stands as a focus of much else in the field.

Ong argues that our knowledge of oral culture is distorted by literacy. We need, therefore, to think ourselves out of literacy and into a purely oral world if we are to be able to understand fully the real significance of literacy itself and the differences entailed when it supersedes orality. The characteristics of the oral world that he discovers using this method are that it is 'formulaic', conservative, 'close to the human lifeworld', 'agonistically toned', empathetic, homeostatic, situational, and involves memorization by formula rather than verbatim. The literate world is the opposite to all of these things: it is abstract, analytic, distancing, objective and separative. The consequence of these differences between orality and literacy is that it becomes possible to distinguish between two major cultural forms in the history of human development – what Ong calls 'verbomotor' cultures and 'high-technology' cultures. The former are word-oriented, the latter object-oriented. The oral world is communal, externalized, less introspective. The explanantion for these differences lies in a basic principle that distinguishes orality as such from literacy as such. This is the fact that sound only exists in its departing, it cannot be held or captured, but is always in process. It is also an 'interior' process. Marks on visual, external surfaces (i.e., writing) are isolating, dissecting, analytical, associated with other senses in a way that sound is not and, crucially, appear able to 'fix' impressions in a way that sound does not.

The consequences of these fundamental differences between sound and vision are that the advent of literacy, with its dependence on the visual, leads to a 'restructuring of consciousness'. Literacy provides for 'context-free language', 'autonomous discourse', and 'analytical thought'. It is essential for the realization of fuller, interior, human potentialities that remain unrealized in the oral world. Like Goody and Watt (1969), Ong sees the possibility that writing provides of laying two 'texts' side by side, thereby generating critical skills, the ability to examine things separately from their social context, the possibility of differentiating between myth and history. Communication becomes less embedded in the social pressures of the immediate moment.

Faced with the grand claims made by Ong for 'literacy', it is obviously crucial to determine just what 'literacy' itself is. Ong addresses this issue directly and answers the question 'What is writing?' with reference to his previous insistence upon the phenomenological nature of sound and sight. 'True' writing is defined as not the representation of things but the representation of sounds. It therefore excludes pictograms, semiotic marks of various kinds, syllabaries, and even the Semitic alphabet, which comes close to 'true' writing but lacks representation for vowel sounds and therefore calls upon exterior knowledge from the reader. The vocalic alphabet was a vital breakthrough in resolving the technical problem of representing sound graphically, because it needed no extra-textual information in order for the reader to decode the signs. It was therefore most remote from the lifeworld, it analyzed sound most abstractly into purely spatial components. It is at this point that Ong's argument moves from an apparently technical analysis of the nature of writing systems to a historical and social analysis of the nature of human mentality. According to Ong (and to similar authors such as Goody and Olson discussed more fully elsewhere in this volume) literacy in such a writing system variously 'enables', 'facilitates', 'fosters', etc., the shift from a 'prelogical' to a 'logical' mentality: the distinction of myth from history, the growth of science, objectivity, critical thought and abstraction. It is on these assumptions that claims regarding 'Western' superiority are founded. Whatever precise linguistic analyses may be embedded within this account of literacy and orality, they are popularly developed in political and ideological terms that assume power to define and shape the world itself.

It is for this reason, rather than simply the 'academic' interest of the analyses, that it is important to pay attention to Ong's work directly. Indirectly it is already likely that it lies beneath many 'folk' assumptions about literacy.

I shall consider Ong's views on three levels: methodological, empirical, and theoretical. The methodology he employs is mainly deductive: it has affinities with the nineteenth-century methodology in social anthropology known as 'if I were a horse' thinking (discussed above in chapter 4), whereby the observer puts himself or herself into the position of the imagined subject. The classic problem with such a method, which ultimately in some form at least remains crucial to any interpretative understanding, arises, when the observer knows nothing about the culture and context of those whose thinking he or she is assuming to represent. In Ong's case, not only does he know little about the rich variety of different cultures that he aggregates together as 'oral', but according to his own argument he cannot ever know about them, since he himself is from a 'literate' culture. If he is right that writing has such deep effects on consciousness as to distort our view of orality, then Ong, too, is trapped in his own literate mentality: an effort of the will, or imagination, seems hardly enough to counteract the profound effects that he himself attributes to this. Where he does appeal to knowledge of actually existing 'oral' socie-ties, he faces two major problems. First, there are few such societies in the present world, since most people have had some contact, however minimal, with forms of literacy, whether in the shape of labels on clothes, street signs, or more formal procedures as found in westernized schooling. More problematic at a methodological level is the problem that Ong appears to want to use present-day 'oral' cultures, if such could be found, as evidence for the nature of *past* societies. This, too, has its roots in nineteenth-century thought, notably that the history of the world was laid out like geological strata and one had only to investigate contemporary 'primitive' societies to find layers of our own past that western society had evolved beyond. Social anthropology in this century has demonstrated that the richness and variety of non-technologically advanced societies should be taken as evidence of the multifarious directions of 'evolution': the unilinear, evolutionary model is no longer tenable and contemporary societies can no longer be viewed as evidence of 'the past'.

There is also a circularity in the arguments used by Ong (and similar authors) when examples are adduced that would disprove their claims for literacy. When Kathleen Gough, for instance, arguing against Goody's insistence on the scientific implications of literacy, points out that literacy in early India did not lead to 'Western-type' science (Gough, 1968), Goody responds that this then must have been a 'restricted' form of literacy (Goody, 1968). By definition, then, most actual literacy practice has been 'restricted' since it has not fulfilled the claims made by these 'great divide' authors. Ong himself argues that where features he ascribes to orality are found still in fully literate societies, then they must be 'residual oral' features. Conversely, where 'literate' features appear in 'oral' societies, they must be due to 'literate' influence. There is no way, within this circular model, of testing the claims put forward.

Finally, it is not clear whether the claims for mental progress are attributable to individual cognitive states or to whole cultures. What, precisely, is the unit of study? Are we concerned with subcultures (which appears to be the case when Ong writes of the importance of certain post-medieval literacy developments), with aspects of all persons, with periods, or with whole eras of human development? The claims appear to be pitched at the highest level, but the arguments slide from one to another.

This also links with the major empirical weakness of the argument. What Ong is claiming for 'literate society' appears to be the particular conventions, beliefs and practices of certain subcultures, most notably the western, academic subculture of which he himself is a part. The 'rationality', 'detachment' and 'objectivity' of the members of this group are, of course, ideals and goals rather than empirical accounts of what they have actually achieved. There is some confusion in treating these aims as though they were empirical evidence for the actual consequences of literacy. Similarly, what empirical evidence we do have from societies with different or less permeating literacies is that they do not necessarily lack the characteristics of 'logic', 'abstraction', etc., that Ong attributes to literacy. Finnegan (1973, 1988) and others (Halverson, 1992a and b) in their accounts of 'oral' literature and anthropologists (Bloch, 1975) describing, for instance, courts of law and political speeches in small-scale societies, have produced ample evidence of these deeper skills. Indeed, it would be surprising if it were otherwise, since these are cornerstones of communicability across cultures and, at their most profound, not subject to cultural variability, whatever variations there may be in surface forms. All people have conventions for formalizing, distancing, analyzing, separating, holding some things constant, acting as if the evanescent world could be 'fixed'.

Having examined some of the methodological and empirical objections to Ong's position and, by association, that of many other writers on literacy, I would finally like to consider some theoretical issues. The primary point of importance here, and which runs through the argument of this book, is that the characteristics which Ong would attribute to literacy are in fact those of the social context and the specific culture in which the literacy being described is located. The emphasis on 'detachment', for instance, is a feature of particular social situations, exemplified perhaps in our culture within certain academic uses of literacy (although not exclusively) and in others through such institutions as courts, public speaking and oral academic discourse. From a theoretical standpoint, it is also incorrect to conceive of 'literacy' in isolation from other media of communication. Literacy practices are always embedded in oral uses, and the variations between cultures are generally variations in the *mix* of oral/literate channels. Even within the academy, Ong's major exemplar of the literate mentality, we find conventions for mixing oral and literate discourse: lectures, seminars, and tutorials are both oral situations and 'literacy events', in Shirley Brice Heath's sense (1983) – the lecture includes literacy both in the hearers taking notes and the deliverer reading the paper, while seminars frequently consist of both discussion and note-taking variously intermixed. The form of speech may well be affected by conventions associated with writing, but conversely the form of *writing* – particularly note-taking and seminars and lectures, discussed already in the introduction – is influenced by the oral context in which it is performed. From a theoretical perspective, then, if we are formulating proposals for research into literate practices, we need to employ a model of communication that takes full account of this mix.

The crux of Ong's claim for literacy was, as we have seen, that it uniquely appears to 'fix' the evanescent nature of sound and of experience. I would argue, however, that language itself already has this quality in its oral dimension, namely of classifying and thereby 'fixing' the continuum of experience. The relationship between a spoken word or a sound and its referent is similar to that which Ong claims is distinctive to the relationship between a written word and its referent: in both cases the signs – whether visual or oral/aural – work at a level of abstraction in representing meaning. Fixing, separation, abstraction all happen without literacy. Furthermore, pictures, ritual, stories all transform the evanescent to the quasi-permanent, distance us from the immediate, heighten consciousness and so forth. Ong would argue that it is the specific nature of the *coding* system – the consistent relationship between signs and sounds – employed in vocalic, alphabetic literacy that distinguishes it from these other forms. In pictographic systems, for instance, the code remains unfixed (there is no consistent relationship between signs and sounds). Likewise, in non-vocalic alphabets where vowels are not indicated by separate letters the coding system is thereby incomplete. It is, however, not clear why Ong should draw the line at this point. Even the vocalic alphabet, in which vowel sounds are indicated as well as consonants, is not a perfect 'coding' system: the context is still necessary to get the sounds right, there is considerable ambiguity as to how a sign or series of signs should be sounded and extra textual information is necessary here too. An alphabetic script locked away for centuries does not immediately reveal its message or indicate to the reader how to sound out the words. It might be claimed that the linguists' system of 'phonetic' writing, used for transcribing oral language more accurately than everyday alphabets can do, comes closest to Ong's ideal of a 'perfect' coding system. But this system too operates within precise and limited conventions and for specific aims. Moreover, no one would claim that the use of such a phonetic writing system has profound implications for cognitive processes – it is just a technical device for doing a particular job. There is, then, a continuum in coding systems and there appears to be no theoretical reason, empirical evidence, or clear methodology that would justify drawing the line between one system and another and then making large claims for cognition, logic, etc., on either side of that line.

Ong's thesis, then, appears to have little value in the investigation of the relationship between orality and literacy. We would do better to look for more specific relationships between literacy events and literacy practices on the one hand, and oral conventions on the other. In the project of investigating these relationships on a cross-cultural basis and in such a way as to yield fruitful generalizations, Ong's thesis does not provide much help and is, indeed, likely to mislead the unwary researcher. And yet it continues to exercise considerable influence, indirect as much as direct, in the field of Literacy Studies. For this reason it is worthy of attention, if only to develop ways of moving beyond it.

References

Bloch, M. (ed.) (1975) *Political Language and Oratory*. Academic Press: London.

Finnegan, R. (1973) 'Literacy Versus Non-Literacy: The Great Divide', in R. Finnegan and B. Horton (eds) *Modes of Thought*. OUP: London.

Finnegan, R. (1988) *Literacy and Orality*. Basil Blackwell: Oxford.

Goody, J. (ed.) (1969) *Literacy in Traditional Societies*. CUP: Cambridge.

Goody, J. and Watt, I. (1969) 'The Consequences of Literacy', in J. Goody (ed.) *Literacy in Traditional Societies*. CUP: Cambridge.

Gough, K. (1968) 'Implications of Literacy in Traditional China and India', in J. Goody (ed.) *Literacy in Traditional Societies*. CUP: Cambridge.

Halverson, J. (1992a) 'Havelock on Greek Orality and Literacy', *Journal of the History of Ideas*, vol. 16, nos 1–3: 148–63.

Halverson, J. (1992b) 'Goody and the Implosion of the Literacy Thesis', *Man*, n.s., vol. 27, no. 2: 301–17.

Heath, S.B. (1983) *Ways with Words*. CUP: Cambridge.

Ong, W. (1982). *Literacy and Orality: The Technologizing of the Word*. Methuen: New York/London.

Street, B. (1984) *Literacy in Theory and Practice*. CUP: Cambridge.

Street, B. (1988) 'Literacy Practices and Literacy Myths', in R. Saljo (ed.) *The Written World*. Springer Press: Berlin/New York.

8 Literacy Practices and Literacy Myths

During the early 1980s there appeared in the USA, a number of collections of academic papers that claimed to represent the relationship between literacy and orality as a 'continuum' rather than, as in much of the previous literature, as a 'divide' (cf. Coulmas and Ehlich, 1983; Frawley, 1982; Olson, Hildyard and Torrance, 1985; Nystrand, 1982; Tannen, 1982b; Wagner, 1983; Whiteman, 1981). It appeared that the differences between literate and oral channels of communication had been overstated in the past and that scholars were now more concerned with overlap, mix and diverse functions in context. I shall examine some of these new representations, and argue that the supposed shift from divide to continuum is more rhetorical than real: that, in fact, many of the writers in this field continue to represent literacy as sufficiently different from orality in its social and cognitive consequences, that their findings scarcely differ from the classic concept of the 'great divide' (cf. Goody, 1977). I shall argue that the implicit persistence of claims that the practitioners themselves would often explicitly reject can be explained with reference to the methodological and theoretical assumptions that underlie their work: in particular a narrow definition of social context, related to the split in linguistics between pragmatics and semantics; the reification of literacy in itself at the expense of recognition of its location in structures of power and ideology, also related to general linguistic assumptions about the 'neutrality' of their object of study; and the restriction of 'meaning' within traditional linguistics to the level of syntax.

I would like to suggest an alternative approach, which would avoid some of the problems generated by these assumptions and which genuinely moves us beyond the great divide. I have outlined above a distinction between 'autonomous' and 'ideological' models of literacy (Street, 1984, 1986, 1987a and b) and I would now like to offer some further clarification (in view of some confusions that have arisen) and to locate the models in the broader context of linguistic and anthropological theory and methodology. In an earlier work (Street, 1984) I distinguished between an autonomous model of literacy, whose exponents studied literacy in its technical aspects, independent of social context, and an ideological model, employed by recent researchers whose concern has been to see literacy practices as inextricably linked to cultural and power structures in a given society. Some critics, such as Myoshi (1988) and Vincent (1986), have taken the distinction to involve an unnecessary polarization and would prefer a synthesis. However, I see the ideological model as itself providing a synthesis between 'technicist' and 'social' approaches, since it avoids the polarization introduced by any attempt to separate out the 'technical' features of literacy, as though the 'cultural bits' could be added on later. It is those who have employed an autonomous model, and who have generally dominated the field of Literacy Studies until recently, who were responsible for setting up a false polarity between the technical and cultural aspects of literacy. The ideological model, on the other hand, does not attempt to deny technical skill or the cognitive aspects of reading and writing, but rather understands them as they are encapsulated within cultural wholes and within structures of power. In that sense the ideological model subsumes rather than excludes the work undertaken within the autonomous model.

I use the term 'ideological' to describe this approach, rather than less contentious or loaded terms such as 'cultural', 'sociological', etc., because it signals quite explicitly that literacy practices are aspects not only of 'culture' but also of power structures. The very emphasis on the 'neutrality' and 'autonomy' of literacy by many writers is ideological in the sense of disguising this power dimension. Any ethnographic account of literacy will, in fact, bring out its significance for power, authority and social differentiation in terms of the author's own interpretation of these concepts. Since all approaches to literacy in practice will involve some such bias, it is better scholarship to admit to and expose the particular ideological framework being employed from the very beginning – it can then be opened to scrutiny, challenged and refined in ways which are more difficult when the ideology remains hidden. This is to use the term 'ideological' not in its old-fashioned Marxist (and current anti-

Marxist) sense of 'false consciousness' and simple-minded dogma, but rather in the sense employed by 'radical' groups within contemporary anthropology, sociolinguistics and cultural studies, where ideology is the site of tension between authority and power on the one hand and individual resistance and creativity on the other (Asad, 1980; Bourdieu, 1976; Hall, Hobson, Lowe and Willis, 1980; Mace, 1979; Strathern, 1985). This tension operates through the medium of a variety of cultural practices, including particularly language and, of course, literacy. It is in this sense that it is important to approach the study of literacy in terms of an explicit ideological model. I would now like to locate that model within the broader context of recent developments in linguistic and anthropological theory and methodology.

Within linguistics there has recently been a shift towards 'discourse' analysis, which takes as the object of study larger units of language than the word or sentence (cf. Benson and Greaves, 1985; Coulthard, 1977; Stubbs, 1983). I will suggest that this trend towards 'discourse' analysis in linguistics could fruitfully link with recent developments of the 'ethnographic' approach within anthropology that take fuller account of theories of power and ideology. I shall briefly cite work from both discourse analysis, such as Blank and Tannen, and from the ethnographic method, such as Heath, and argue that they provide a useful basis from which to construct a synthesis that develops beyond either approach in isolation. With respect to research in orality and literacy this merging of disciplines and methodologies, within an ideological as opposed to an autonomous model of literacy, provides, I would argue, a means to replace the concept of the great divide with richer, and less ethnocentric concepts. In particular I would like to employ and develop further the concepts of 'literacy events' (Heath, 1982), 'literacy practices' (Street, 1984) and 'communicative practices' (Grillo, 1986).

Heath defines a 'literacy event' as 'any occasion in which a piece of writing is integral to the nature of participants' interactions and their interpretive processes' (Heath, 1982). I employ 'literacy practices' as a broader concept, pitched at a higher level of abstraction and referring to both behaviour and conceptualizations related to the use of reading and/or writing. Literacy practices incorporate not only 'literacy events', as empirical occasions to which literacy is integral, but also 'folk models' of those events and the ideological preconceptions that underpin them. Grillo has extended this notion still further to the notion of communicative practices in general, which obviously owes much to Hymes' work on the 'ethnography of communication' (Hymes, 1974). Grillo construes the concept of communicative practices as including 'the social activities through which language or communication is produced', 'the way in which these activities are embedded in institutions, settings or domains which in turn are implicated in other, wider, social, economic, political and cultural processes' and 'the ideologies, which may be linguistic or other, which guide processes of communicative production' (Grillo, 1986, p. 8). For Grillo, then, 'literacy is seen as one type of communicative practice', within this larger social context, moving the emphasis away from attempts to attribute grand consequences to a particular medium or channel.

Central to development of this conceptual apparatus for the study of literacy is a re-evaluation of the importance of 'context' in linguistic analysis. Linguists, with some justification, have been reluctant to allow the floodwaters of 'social context' to breach defences provided by the rigour and logic of their enterprise. They sense that 'context' is so unbounded and loose that it would swamp their own very precise and bounded studies. One explanation for this fear might be that, whereas linguists recognize the need for rigorous theory and method in studying grammar and syntax, they see the 'social' as something that anyone can comment upon without the need for academic discipline: as Chomsky argued, it is simply 'commonsense' (Chomsky, 1986). For these and other reasons, many linguists have attempted to exclude context altogether from their domain. Grillo, Pratt and Street point out, in an article on anthropology, linguistics and language, that Lyons' well-known distinction between three main levels of analysis: word-meaning, sentence-meaning and utterance-meaning, assumes that the first two are 'to a high degree context independent' (Lyons, 1981, p. 23; cited in Grillo, Pratt and Street, 1987, p. 269). Even when linguists have paid attention to social context, it has been in terms of a narrow definition:

> In linguistics the term *social* tends to be reserved for personal interaction, whereas most anthropologists would want to emphasise that even the native speaker intuiting is a social being. . . .
>
> [Furthermore] when in the analysis of utterance meaning, attention is turned to the social context, the main focus of enquiry has been

> pragmatics, doing things with words. This is undoubtedly an impor-
> tant area of enquiry, and at least one anthropologist (Bloch) has
> recently made extensive use of the concept of illocutionary force.
> However, this should not diminish the attention paid to social context
> in the analysis of the use of language to make propositions about the
> world, since this is also fundamentally a social process. (Ibid., p. 270)

When they do turn to sociology for assistance in the analysis of
'context', linguists have tended to borrow mainly from 'network'
theory, or from Goffman-inspired 'interactionalism', which refers
only to those aspects of context that are directly observable and to
such immediate links between individuals as their 'roles', obligations,
'face-to-face encounters', etc. This is true for post-Firthian linguistics
which, for all its emphasis on language in context, is still bound by
its inheritance from Malinowski of his narrow conception of 'context
of situation', along with the problems of his functionalism that have
been largely superseded by subsequent theoretical developments
within social anthropology (cf. Bailey, 1985). In his book on pragmatics, for instance, Levinson explictly and self-consciously excludes
wider interpretations of 'context' and admits:

> A relatively narrow range of contextual factors and their linguistic
> correlates are considered here: context in this book includes only some
> of the basic parameters of the context of utterance, including partici-
> pants' identity, role and location, assumptions about what participants
> know or take for granted, the place of an utterance within a sequence
> of turns at taking and so on. (Levinson, 1983, p. x)

He does acknowledge the existence of wider interpretations of
'context':

> We know, in fact that there are a number of additional contextual
> parameters that are systematically related to linguistic organisation,
> particularly principles of social interaction of various sorts of both a
> culture specific kind (see e.g., Keenan, 1976) and universal kind (see
> e.g., Brown & Levinson, 1987 [sic 1978]). (Ibid.)

But he excludes them because his aim is to represent faithfully the
philosophico-linguistic tradition in the USA and the UK, rather than,
for instance, that on the continent where the tradition he notes is

'altogether broader' (p. ix) (cf. also Dillon, Coleman, Fahnestock and Agar, 1985, and Bailey, 1985, for explorations of developments in post-Firthian linguistics, particularly with regard to discourse analysis and pragmatics).

I would like to argue that the analysis of the relationship between orality and literacy requires attention to the 'wider parameters' of context largely under-emphasized in Anglo-American linguistics. Within social anthropology, for instance, these would be taken to include the study of kinship organization, conceptual systems, political structures, habitat and economy etc., which are seen as 'systems', and analyzed in terms of function and structure rather than simply of 'network' or 'interaction'. There is little point, according to this perspective, in attempting to make sense of a given utterance or discourse in terms only of its immediate 'context of utterance', unless one knows the broader social and conceptual framework that gives it meaning. This involves not just commonsense, but the development of theories and methods as rigorous as those employed in other domains. It is these theories and methods that provide some guarantee that attention to social context need not swamp or drown the precise aspects of language use selected for study within linguistics.

In recent years the methods and theories employed to study social life in cross-cultural perspective have been subject to rigorous criticism. In contrast with the static, functionalist approach implied in, for instance, Malinowski's 'context of situation', recent approaches within anthropology have emphasized the dynamic nature of social processes and the broader structure of power relations. This has frequently taken the form of exploration of the concept of ideology and of discourse (see Agar, 1986; Agar and Hobbs, 1983; Asad, 1980; Bloch, 1986; Grillo et al., 1987; Parkin, 1984; Strathern, 1985). In this sense 'discourse' refers to the complex of conceptions, classifications and language use that characterize a specific sub-set of an ideological formation. It borrows something from Foucault's usage, although that refers to whole periods of European history, whereas the anthropological usage is often more specific with reference to a given subculture of the scale normally investigated through ethnographic method. This sense of discourse, however, remains rather broader than that normally employed within linguistics, where it frequently indicates (cf. Fairclough, 1992) simply chunks of language larger than the sentence. The boundaries between the senses of the term in the different disciplines remain unclear and can frequently overlap.

Far from being a source of confusion, however, this ambiguity may be turned to constructive use, providing a means to pursue issues that are perhaps harder to grasp within the language and definitions of either discipline separately.

Recent developments in discourse analysis within linguistics, for instance, such as Brown and Yule's concern to 'link thickly described discourse to larger patterns of action and interaction' (quoted in Dillon et al., 1985, p. 456) provide a method which can be more sensitive to language in use than traditional ethnography has been. The method, however, needs to be allied with a linguistic theory that conceives of language as essentially a social process, and which takes full account of more sophisticated theories of language than simple interactionalism, network analysis or commonsense. Similarly, the methods employed by anthropologists do not on their own guarantee theoretical sophistication: it is possible, for instance, for ethnographic accounts of literacy to be conducted within the autonomous model, with all the problems and flaws that entails. However, when ethnographic method is allied to contemporary anthropological theory, emphasizing ideological and power processes and dynamic rather than static models, then it can be more sensitive to social context than either linguistics in general or discourse analysis in particular have tended to be. It is at the interface between these linguistic and anthropological theories on the one hand, and between discourse and ethnographic method on the other, that I envisage future research in the field of Literacy Studies being conducted. This should enable us to replace previous accounts of literacy, based on inadequate methods and theories, with accounts that provide a firm basis for sound cross-cultural comparison and generalization. Until then, we would be well advised to refrain from generalizations, particularly those of the grandiose sort indulged by writers like Ong and Goody, but also even the more modest claims being made within some of the 'collections' on literacy published in the 1980s.

I would now like to examine some of these 'modest' claims more closely and to suggest that, through their reliance on traditional methods and theories regarding the study of literacy, they are still implicitly embedded in the great divide framework that many of their exponents would wish explicitly to reject. I will discuss here a number of these 'literacy myths' as they are particularly important in the arguments put forward in the Sections on Education and Development above: the notion that written discourse encodes meaning through lexicalization and grammar, while oral discourse does so through paralinguistic features, leading to consequential differences between the potential of the two mediums and to an implicit reinstatement of the great divide; the notion that written discourse is more 'connected' and 'cohesive', while oral discourse is fragmentary and disconnected; and finally the myth that written language delivers its meaning directly via the 'words on the page', whereas oral language is more 'embedded' in the immediate social pressures of face-to-face communication.

These myths are both rejected and revived in a collection of essays edited by Deborah Tannen entitled *Spoken and Written Language: Exploring Orality and Literacy* (1982b). In the preface Tannen signals the contemporary trend away from traditional linguistic approaches to literacy:

> Many of the papers in the present collection owe much to the insight of anthropological and literary work on orality and literacy. However, they go beyond this dichotomy to investigate the characteristics and effects of changing traditions, and to suggest that distinctions between orality and literacy on the one hand, and spoken vs. written language on the other, do not suffice to characterize real discourse. For one thing, there are various oral and literate traditions, and there are different ways of realizing these in both spoken and written language.... A number of the chapters consider the relationship of literary to conversational language and find them closer and distinctions between them foggier, than had previously been thought. (Tannen, 1982b, pp. xi–xii)

Similarly in 'The Myth of Orality and Literacy', which was published in another collection of essays on literacy at this time, Tannen challenges two 'myths' of literacy that have been prominent in linguistics: the myth '1) that writing is decontextualised and 2) that text-focused discourse is found only in writing' (1982a, p. 41).

The theory of a great divide between literacy and orality was generally under attack at this time and one might have looked to the many collections of essays being published in the field to develop alternative positions. And yet Tannen herself is typical of many contributors in her tendency to reintroduce the notion, albeit in 'softer' guise. She relates, for instance, how she found 'the notion of oral vs. literate tradition – or more precisely, an oral/literate continuum reflecting relative focus on involvement vs. content – useful to my own research on discourse'. Despite her reference to 'discourse' here, Tannen's account does not represent the shift away from the traditional view of literacy that I am suggesting could be facilitated by a combination of recent discourse analysis with those versions of the ethnographic method that are rooted in theories of power and ideology. Her use of the term remains closer to traditional, and narrower aspects of linguistic theory and method and does little to detach her from the autonomous model of literacy. Her association of orality with 'involvement' and literacy with content in practice replicates classic features of great divide thinking and her use of it cannot help but revive the dichotomy even amidst protestations to the contrary. I would like to pursue here just one strand of her argument, in which she relates the distinction between 'involvement' and 'content' to a further supposed difference between orality and literacy, which she terms 'the cohesion hypothesis'.

'Spoken discourse', according to Tannen, 'establishes cohesion through paralinguistic features whereas written discourse does so through lexicalisation' (1982a, p. 41). In speaking, Tannen argues, paralinguistic features, such as tone, facial expression, etc., reveal the speaker's attitude towards the message and serve to establish cohesion, that is, to show the relationship between ideas, highlight relative importance, etc. 'One cannot speak without showing one's attitude to the message and the speech activity' (1982a, p. 41). In writing, by contrast, 'features of nonverbal and paralinguistic channels are not available' (ibid.). The writer may wrinkle his or her face but it does not show up on the written page. So the relationship between ideas and the writer's attitude to them must be lexicalized. This is done through choice of words, by explicit statements and by conjunctions and subordinate clauses, which do the work that in speaking is done by paralinguistic means. The implications of these differences are that speaking exhibits greater attention to the involvement of participants, while in writing there is a greater emphasis on the content of what is said. However, this does not mean that individuals or groups can be simply labelled either 'oral' or 'literate': 'Rather, people have at their disposal and are inclined to use, based on individual habits as well as social conventions, strategies associated with either or both in speech and writing' (Tannen, 1982a, p. 47).

Some research she conducted on middle-class dinner parties in the USA shows how some participants may employ 'literate-like' strategies in their conversation, while others are employing 'oral-like' stategies, leading to miscommunication and mutual dissatisfaction. For instance, one group which she labels 'literate-like', want the emphasis in stories to be placed upon content and the point to be made explicit, while the other 'oral-like' group dwell upon personal details and emotions and want the point to be inferred from the dramatic structure rather than stated explicitly. The two groups also have trouble over turn-taking and sequence: the oral-like ones frequently talk at the same time while the literate-like group prefer one person at a time to talk and will themselves halt the flow of conversation by refusing their turn and remaining silent if they are 'interrupted'.

The justification for applying the labels 'oral-like' and 'literate-like', which slide into simply 'oral' and 'literate' at times, is that the groups exhibit features that are associated with orality and literacy according to the cohesion hypothesis. Waiting one's turn, for instance, is literate-like or literate in the sense that it involves putting emphasis on the content of what is said, while overlapping is oral in the sense of emphasizing personal involvement, at the expense of 'the clear relay of information'. Those who prefer 'explicitness' are literate in the sense that the cohesion hypothesis shows writing to require more explicitness, through lexicalization and syntax, whereas those who prefer the message to be inferred, or conveyed by other than direct verbal expression, are oral-like in the sense, again according to the cohesion hypothesis, that oral communication places more emphasis on paralinguistic means of conveying the feelings of the speakers.

These claims seem to me to be fairly dubious and are of a kind with the myths of literacy that Tannen herself rightly rejects. The persistence of such myths derives, I would suggest, from the underlying methodological and theoretical framework. The argument that writing does not exhibit features of 'nonverbal and paralinguistic channels', for instance, derives from viewing written production within a narrow definition of 'social context'. If we approach 'context' in the broad sense suggested above, where discourse analysis and ethnography overlap, and where the methods are rooted in theories of power and ideology and of language as essentially social, then the characteristics of written channels of communication will appear somewhat different. We will find, for instance, a whole range of paralinguistic features by which meaning is expressed through writing, at least as complex and rich as those of oral discourse. To take an example close to home: when a piece of writing appears in an academic journal, its standing and the attitude the reader brings to it rests on more than 'lexicalization' alone: the status of the journal itself, even the quality and style of the paper and covers, all contribute to the 'meaning' of the propositions contained within it and to the degree of attention it is deemed to deserve from an 'academic' reader on the one hand or, on the other, whether it is worth a 'lay' person bothering with it at all. A neatly bound and well-produced book with a Cambridge University Press imprint gets different attention than a scruffy pile of A4 computer paper, even though the lexicalization in both cases may be exactly the same. To take an example from further afield, Bledsoe and Robey (1986) describe how the Mende of Sierra Leone impart meaning to written products in a variety of ways:

> Writing has secondary means for communicating meanings other than those literally transcribed on the paper. Elegant paper, typewritten script, and a clean, multicoloured airmail envelope are signs of respect for the person addressed as well as for enhancing the prestige of the message. Conversely, if the writer wishes to show disrespect, he might write the message in red ink (an insult). (Bledsoe and Robey, 1986, p. 225)

The 'secondary means' described here are precisely those paralinguistic and non-verbal features that Tannen and others find only in oral discourse. Bledsoe and Robey, in fact, show how the message may be the same orally or in writing but the very act of sending it in written form itself indicates something about the message:

> Writing often substitutes for speech, even when the latter might just as well communicate a direct message. The Mende frequently approach someone of high status for a favour by handing him a written letter. This circumvents face-to-face 'shame' on the part of the supplicant, even if he delivers his own message in person, as he often does. Although in some instances writing may enhance communication by avoiding stuttering and embarrassing pauses, the Mende emphasise that writing is intended to enhance the importance of a message and to show that the sender feels respect for the receiver. (Ibid., p. 224)

Shame, respect and status, then, may all be conveyed by paralinguistic features of writing: the furrow on the brow of the writer or the bow towards the receiver can be enscribed despite Tannen's claim that they 'will not show up on the written page' (Tannen, 1982b, p. 41): they show up in the fact and nature of the sending and may, in her terms, be encoded in other than lexical features of the message. Bledsoe's and Robey's work also suggests more subtle and less obvious features of writing as a means of establishing secrecy and maintaining control of, or, as they put it, 'managing' knowledge. Among the Mende, secret societies represent an important unofficial source of social standing, particularly among women. Entry and progression through higher levels of one of these secret societies may be determined by a series of rituals and thresholds, and, among these, writing plays an important part. Writing is absorbed by Mende secret societies into a tradition of secrecy and exclusion, where hierarchies of access to knowledge maintain degrees of power and control over others. We cannot really claim to make sense of items of script produced within this framework if we attend only to the meaning of the 'words on the page' and to the lexical devices for encoding meaning: these represent only one aspect, Bledsoe and Robey suggest, of the 'potential' of writing and to ignore others is to miss much of what gives it meaning in 'real-life' situations. Observation of these, moreover, is to be understood not simply in terms of the immediate context of utterance but of such broader features of social and cultural life as the secret societies of the Mende and their institutional control and definition of hierarchies of power. It is, then, this broader meaning of the term 'context' to which Bledsoe and Robey are referring when they argue for understanding literacy.

> Writing is assuredly a medium of great potential in social interaction, but we underscore that different social uses of writing are culturally limited or enhanced in different societies. In itself writing does not mechanically produce social results. The cultural context greatly influences the social role of writing, both as a mode of communication and as a type of knowledge. By treating literacy as a resource in this way, moreover, we de-emphasize the dichotomy of speech versus writing. . . . We view the two modes as more similar than different in their sociological impact . . . (and so much of the discussion) could apply to oral competence as well. (Ibid., p. 203)

This stress on the similarity, rather than the difference, between written and oral discourse is also brought out by another recent study that makes explicit the extent to which it was the methodological framework of traditional linguistics that helped reinforce the myth of the great divide. Marion Blank (1982), in an article on pre-school language use, examines a number of characteristics classically attributed to literacy and which have frequently been used to emphasize a great divide between written and spoken language, notably that literacy is 'disembedded', 'sustained and sequential', and has 'implicit connectedness'. These assumptions, she suggests, derived from the traditional linguistic method of decoding separate components of an utterance – the 'context independence' of word and sentence meaning cited from Lyons above. This led to the study of oral language as consisting of separate chunks or fragments, often 'imperfectly grammatical', as though it lacked cohesion and connectedness. Written language, on the other hand, was studied in larger chunks in which a thread could be discerned running through the parts. From this it appeared to follow that literacy was intrinscally characterized by connectedness and cohesion and orality by fragmentation. However, Blank notes that recent research in linguistics has shifted away from the methodology that helped sustain such distinctions, and towards analysis of organized, connected text or discourse, whether oral or written, and this has considerable implications for traditional assumptions about orality and literacy. By applying discourse analysis to oral production it is beginning to become apparent that there are implicit rules of cohesion that were missed by the previous, atomistic methodology. Conversation analysis, for instance, focuses on 'the structure and cohesion rules that make a chunk of talk "a conversation"' (Blank, 1982; cf. also Craig and Tracy, 1983). Blank gives examples where children's talk was tape recorded and later analysis showed how early references in a discussion were sustained in later comments:

> For example, in a lunchtime conversation between a mother and her 5-year-old child, the mother said, 'Now eat your carrots'. Then she paused and, changing tone, said 'Oh, I forgot to plant the tomatoes'. The conversation continued for a while and suddenly the child altered the flow by saying 'I know why you said tomatoes. When you said carrots, it made you think of tomatoes, and that's why you did it'. (Blank, 1982, p. 85)

Blank interprets this as demonstrating that 'the child was saying she expects a conversation to be connected, that the grouping of tomatoes and carrots in that context was peculiar but that there must be some logic available by which that combination could be explained – and indeed, she found the logic' (loc. cit.). Oral discourse, then, may be more 'cohesive' than previously assumed, if only we were to study it in an appropriate way. 'Cohesion' may not be such an important criterion for distinguishing oral from written language as many earlier researchers had assumed.

On the one hand, as Blank says, oral discourse studied in this way may turn out to be more cohesive than previously assumed. On the other hand, we may also need to examine more closely the assumed intrinsic cohesiveness of written production. The examples that linguists tend to use, and that Blank herself employs, are most often drawn from 'literary' writing, or from the 'essay-text' tradition. These, of course, have a 'built-in' cohesion since the conventions by which they are written require a thread of connectedness throughout a whole piece and since they are usually written by a single author whose own presence sustains and implicitly links the parts. There are, however, many other uses of literacy in everyday life, and those to which the majority of people are exposed most of the time do not belong to this particular tradition: they consist, rather, of apparent fragments – signs, labels, lists, advertizements, etc. There is a cohesion to these too, but it is not to be found at the overt level of the authored script but at deeper levels of culture and ideology, levels missed by traditional linguistic methodology, with its tendency to dwell on a particular, culture-specific form of literary writing.

Since the discourse methodology that will provide insights into these submerged levels of cohesion in writing and in oral discourse alike is only relatively recent, there is consequently little comparative data available on which to make general claims for difference between orality and literacy based on this feature. It is therefore unsound on empirical as well on theoretical grounds to use 'cohesion' as a criterion for contrasts between orality and literacy as such. The cohesion hypothesis is another literacy myth.

If both oral and literate practices are frequently part of a sustained narrative whose connections lie deep in the culture, so that it is difficult for them to be observed at the overt level or in the immediate context, then what methodological framework can be employed to investigate them? Blank's article suggests that the shift towards discourse analysis within linguistics offers a useful beginning. The analysis of deeper levels of discourse cohesion and communicative exchange in both oral and literate modes also requires, I would suggest, an extension of discourse analysis into an ethnographic approach, such as represented in the work of Shirley Brice Heath. I will conclude with a brief discussion of how the concepts and methods she employs can be extended to provide a basis for the kind of literacy studies that I am proposing.

Heath's work challenges, in particular, a further myth of literacy generated by traditional linguistic methodology, that is, the assumed autonomy of written language, where the meaning is taken to reside in 'the autonomous text' (Olson, 1977, p. 268). Oral language, in contrast, was seen as quintessentially a social exchange, in which any 'true' or unambiguous meaning was usually swamped by the social pressures exerted by the participants' relative status, power, etc. These arguments are dealt with in various chapters of this book, notably chapter 7, which focuses on the version of them to be found in Walter Ong's work, and chapter 4, where the debates within anthropology in particular are discussed more fully. For present purposes, I am concerned to draw attention to the ways in which recent work at the interface of linguistics and anthropology has also challenged this myth and suggested a methodology for studying similarities between orality and literacy in relation to features traditionally taken as indicative of a great divide.

Heath (1983), for instance, has employed an ethnographic approach to demonstrate how written language as well as oral can work as a form of exchange in situations of face-to-face communication. The Piedmont people she studied may open a letter on their verandahs and discuss its meaning with friends and neighbours, constructing a reply in collaboration (see also Shuman, 1983, on 'collaborative literacy'). The links and underlying cohesion of the reading and of the writing in this situation derive from the interaction of the participants rather than being the product of a single 'author', composing in isolation. Written language, then, cannot be divided from oral language on the grounds that it lacks the quality of immediate exchange characteristic of face-to-face communication. Moreover the situation that she describes where Piedmont people are negotiating the meaning of a letter is part of a larger 'context' than the immediate one of the participants' interaction on the verandah: to understand it requires further knowledge of the culture and ideology of the participants and of a range of other literacy events and practices in which they engage than simply those under immediate scrutiny. A crucial feature of this broader context is relations of power between the various participants. 'Official' letters often represent an exercise of power over the recipient, in this case a school board determining where a child will be sent, while delivery of a response may represent a form of local autonomy and resistance to central dictates. The words on the page do not carry independent meaning but depend upon their location in this power struggle for their active meaning: the literacy events that can be observed as letters arrive, are read and replied to, are part of a larger literacy practice that includes local/state relations, and broad ideological assumptions about the 'power' of the written word, that are less easily observed or described empirically. The participants themselves take these into account in interpreting and constructing the 'meaning' of written items but it has proved difficult for autonomous linguistics to do so due to its insistence that language and literacy can be studied independently of this level of social context.

Recent work at the interface of anthropology and linguistics, discourse and ethnography, however, has provided a way out of this difficulty by challenging the myths of orality and literacy that have dominated research in this area for too long. Literacy, it is now apparent, cannot be divided from orality on the grounds either of cohesion, or of connectedness or that it employs paralinguistic as opposed to lexical features of language. Nor is it true to suggest that oral language is more embedded in social situations and 'exchange', while written language remains independent and autonomous. The attention to these supposed differences between literacy and orality that helped sustain belief in the great divide, even when its grosser features were being rejected, can now itself be seen as a product of traditional linguistic methodology and of the cultural conventions of the linguists themselves. The chapters above, while attempting to free us from some of these restrictive traditions and conventions, represent, then, mainly an attempt to build on the positive work in the field of linguistics, anthropology and education cited there in order to suggest new directions for literacy research and practice.

References

Agar, M. (1986) *Independents Declared*. Smithsonian: Washington.
Agar, M. and Hobbs, J. (1983) 'Natural Plans: Using AI Planning in the Analysis of Ethnographic Interviews', *Ethos*, vol. 11: 33–48.

Apple, M. (ed.) (1982) *Cultural and Economic Reproduction in Education.* Routledge & Kegan Paul: London.

Asad, T. (1980) 'Anthropology and the Analysis of Ideology', *Man*, n.s., vol. 14, no. 4: 604–27.

Bailey, R.W. (1985) 'Negotiation and Meaning: Revisiting the "Context of Situation"', in J.D. Benson and W.S. Greaves (eds) *Systemic Functional Approaches to Discourse.* Ablex: Norwood, New Jersey.

Benson, J.D. and Greaves, W.S. (eds) (1985) *Systemic Functional Approaches to Discourse.* Ablex: Norwood, New Jersey.

Blank, M. (1982) 'Language and School Failure: Some Speculations About the Relationship Between Oral and Written Language', in L. Feagans and D. Farran (eds) *The Language of Children Reared in Poverty.* Academic Press: New York.

Bledsoe, C. and Robey, K. (1986) 'Arabic Literacy and Secrecy among the Mende of Sierra Leone', *Man*, n.s., vol. 21, no. 2: 202–26.

Bloch, M. (ed.) (1975) *Political Language and Oratory.* Academic Press: London.

Bloch, M. (1986, June) 'Literacy and Enlightenment', in K. Schousboe and M.T. Larsen (eds) *Literacy and Society.* Akademsig Forlag: Copenhagen.

Bourdieu, P. (1976) 'Systems of Education and Systems of Thought', in R. Dale, G. Esland and M. MacDonald (eds) *Schooling and Capitalism.* Open University/Routledge & Kegan Paul: London.

Brown, P. and Levinson, S. (1987) *Politeness: Some Universals in Language Usage, Studies in International Sociolinguistics*, vol. 4. CUP: Cambridge.

Chomsky, N. (1986) 'Changing Perspectives on the Nature of Acquisition of Language', Keynote Address, 11th Annual Boston University Conference on Language Development. Boston, Massachusetts, 17–19 October.

Coulmas, F. and Ehlich, K. (eds) (1983) *Writing in Focus.* Mouton: New York.

Coulthard, M. (1977) *An Introduction to Discourse Analysis.* Longman: London.

Craig, R. and Tracy, K. (1983) *Conversational Coherence: Form, Structure and Strategy.* Sage: London.

Dillon, G., Coleman, L., Fahnestock, J. and Agar M. (1985) 'Review Article of Discourse Analysis and Pragmatics', *Language*, vol. 69: 446–60.

Fairclough, N. (1992) *Discourse and Social Change.* Polity Press: London.

Frawley, W. (ed.) (1982) *Linguistics and Literacy.* Proceedings of the Delaware Symposium on Language Studies. Plenum: New York.

Goody, J. (1977) *Domestication of the Savage Mind.* CUP: Cambridge.

Grillo, R. (1986, April) 'Aspects of Language and Class', paper presented at Lancaster Conference on Linguistics and Politics.

Grillo, R., Pratt, J. and Street, B. (1987) 'Anthropology, Linguistics and

Language', in J. Lyons (ed.) *New Horizons in Linguistics*, vol. 2. Penguin: London.

Hall, S., Hobson, D., Lowe, A. and Willis, P. (eds) (1980) *Culture, Media, Language*. Hutchinson: London.

Heath, S.B. (1982) 'What No Bedtime Story Means: Narrative Skills at Home and at School', *Language in Society*, vol. 11: 49–76.

Heath, S.B. (1983) *Ways with Words*. CUP: Cambridge.

Hymes, D. (ed.) (1964) *Language in Culture and Society*. Harper & Row: New York.

Hymes, D. (1974) *Foundations in Sociolinguistics: an Ethnographic Approach*. University of Pennsylvania Press: Philadelphia.

Keenan, E.L. (1976) 'The Universality of Conversational Implicature', *Language in Society*, vol. 5: 67–80.

Levinson, S. (1983) *Pragmatics*. CUP: Cambridge.

Lyons, J. (1981) *Language, Meaning and Context*. Fontana: London.

Mace, J. (1979) *Working with Words*. Chameleon: London.

Myoshi, M. (1988) 'The "Great Divide" Once Again: Problematics of the Novel and the Third World', in *Culture and History*, vol. 3. Museum Tusculanum Press: Copenhagen.

Nystrand, M. (ed.) (1982) *What Writers Know: the Language, Process and Structure of Written Discourse*. Academic Press: New York.

Olson, D. (1977) 'From Utterance to Text: the Bias of Language in Speech and Writing', *Harvard Educational Review*, vol. 47: 254–79.

Olson, D., Hildyard, A. and Torrance, N. (eds) (1985) *Literacy, Language and Learning*. CUP: Cambridge.

Parkin, D. (1984) 'Political Language', *Annual Review of Anthropology*, vol. 13: 345–65.

Shuman, A. (1983) 'Collaborative Literacy in an Urban, Multi-ethnic Neighbourhood', in D. Wagner (ed.) *Literacy and Ethnicity. International Journal of the Sociology of Language*, vol. 42: 69–81.

Strathern, M. (1985) 'Feminism and Anthropology', unpublished manuscript.

Street, B. (1984) *Literacy in Theory and Practice*. CUP: Cambridge.

Street, B. (1986) 'Walter Ong on Literacy', *Aspects*, vol. 1: 2–16.

Street, B. (1987a) 'Literacy and Social Change: the Significance of Social Context in the Development of Literacy Programmes', in D. Wagner (ed.) *The Future of Literacy in a Changing World*. Pergamon Press: Oxford.

Street, B. (1987b) 'Literacy and Orality as Ideological Constructions: Some Problems in Cross-Cultural Studies', in M. Harbsmeier and M. T. Larsen (eds) *Cultural History*, vol. 2. University of Copenhagen: Copenhagen.

Stubbs, M. (1983) *Discourse Analysis*. University of Chicago Press: Chicago.

Tannen, D. (1982a) 'The Myth of Orality and Literacy', in W. Frawley (ed.) *Linguistics and Literacy*. Proceedings of the Delaware Symposium on Language Studies. Plenum: New York.

Tannen, D. (ed.) (1982b) *Spoken and Written Language: Exploring Orality and Literacy*. Ablex: Norwood, New Jersey.

Vincent, D. (1986) 'Review of "Literacy in Theory and Practice", Brian V. Street, Cambridge University Press 1984 and "Literacy, Language and Learning", eds, David, R. Olson, Nancy Torrance and Angela Hildyard, Cambridge University Press 1985', *Sociological Review*, vol. 34, no. 4: 897–9.

Wagner, D. (ed.) (1983) *Literacy and Ethnicity. International Journal of the Sociology of Language*, vol. 42.

Whiteman, M. (ed.) (1981) *Writing: the Nature, Development and Teaching of Written Communication. Vol. 1. Variation in Writing: Functional and Linguistic and Cultural Differences*. Erlbaum: New Jersey.

Index